From Zero to Viral

An Influencer's Journey

Olivia Sterling

Foreword

Welcome to the world of social media influence, where creativity, honesty, and connection join together to create the digital environment. We go on a trip in this book to discover the secrets of being a successful social media influencer and harnessing the great potential of this modern phenomena.

The chapters included inside these pages hold the keys to comprehending the complexities of social media and its revolutionary influence on our lives. We'll talk about the emergence of social media influencers and how to create a personal brand that captivates and connects with your target audience. We go into the basic building blocks of constructing an appealing online presence, from recognizing your distinct value proposition to cultivating an authentic voice.

We will walk you through the process of analyzing several social media sites, selecting your major platforms, and researching supplemental channels that compliment your content strategy. Our investigation continues with insights into developing captivating content that captivates, informs, and inspires. We will explore the art of storytelling and discover the secrets of harnessing images and aesthetics to increase the impact of your brand.

Building an active community is important to social media impact, and we'll look at how to determine your target audience, tactics for improving participation, and the value of cooperation and networking. Creating engaging biographies and profiles, using keywords and hashtags, and improving discoverability and search engine optimization can help you optimize your social media profiles for success.

Partnerships with brands give up new opportunities, and we will look at how to approach collaborations, negotiate contracts and pay, and preserve authenticity in brand partnerships. We will then use affiliate marketing and sponsorships to increase your impact while adhering to transparency and ethical issues.

creating your own products and services is a thrilling prospect, and we will walk you through the process of generating lucrative ideas, creating and launching your offers, and managing e-commerce and delivery. We will look at essential indicators, analytics tools, and the art of modifying plans based on findings to help you gauge your success and make data-driven decisions.

Staying relevant and adjusting to algorithm changes is critical as social media evolves. We will teach you how to stay on top of social media trends and increase your reach outside the digital sphere. Building a strong personal brand is essential for success, and we will look at growing your online presence, establishing your brand identity, and communicating genuinely with your audience.

We will go into the complexities of understanding this strong technique, addressing influencers strategically, and analyzing the performance of your influencer campaigns in the domain of influencer marketing. In addition, we will explore the emergence of video content, provide insights into generating captivating videos, and use live video and streaming to engage with your audience in real-time.

You will receive vital knowledge, practical advice, and inspiration from each chapter as you begin on your own journey to become a social media influencer. This book will be your guide to navigating this changing terrain, whether you're a fledgling artist, an aspiring entrepreneur, or a brand trying to unleash the potential of social media impact.

Now, enter this realm of limitless possibilities. Embrace your own voice, fire your creativity, and harness the power of social media influence to leave an unforgettable imprint on the digital landscape. The adventure awaits, and the possibilities are limitless. Let us go on this wonderful journey of impact and inspiration together.

Summary

Chapter 1: Understanding the Power of Social Media

The Rise of Social Media Influencers

In recent years, the growth of social media influencers has been a huge phenomena, affecting how people interact with online platforms and shaping the digital environment. Individuals have grasped the chance to share their opinions, ideas, and experiences with a worldwide audience with the emergence of Web 2.0 and the rising accessibility of social media platforms.

Individuals may promote their abilities, experience, and lifestyles on social media sites such as Instagram, YouTube, TikTok, and Twitter. Influencers have emerged as major people with large followings and strong influence over their audiences. They've developed personal brands and communities around their content, which ranges from beauty and fashion to fitness, travel, and cuisine.

Influencers are distinguished by their ability to engage with their followers on a personal level. Influencers, unlike traditional celebrities, are frequently perceived as personable and approachable. They interact with their audience through honest and often uncensored material, revealing peeks into their everyday lives, offering advice, and developing trusting and authentic connections.

Social media influencers' effect extends beyond just entertainment or inspiration. Their suggestions, product ratings, and endorsements have a strong influence on customer behavior. Followers regard influencers as reliable sources of information and seek their advice when making purchase decisions. As a result, influencer marketing has grown in popularity, in which corporations collaborate with influencers to promote their products or services to a highly engaged and focused audience.

Influencers have used their internet presence to develop profitable careers. They make money through a variety of means, including as brand collaborations, sponsored content, affiliate marketing, and the development of their own products or services. Because of the financial possibilities, many people have chosen to work as social media influencers, creating a highly competitive field.

While the rise of social media influencers has created tremendous benefits, it has also created significant obstacles. Influencers are under pressure to provide interesting and high-quality material on a continuous basis, maintain their online reputation, and stay relevant in a fast-paced digital world. They are also responsible for utilizing their influence responsibly and publicly, revealing brand partnerships, and retaining their audience's confidence.

Social media influencers have also had a huge impact on popular culture. They have reshaped aesthetic standards, launched trends, and increased the visibility of social problems. Their reach goes beyond the internet arena, as they frequently cooperate with businesses, feature in conventional media, and become sought-after individuals in a variety of sectors.

In recent years, the growth of social media influencers has been a huge phenomena, affecting how people interact with online platforms and shaping the digital environment. Individuals have grasped the chance to share their opinions, ideas, and experiences with a worldwide audience with the emergence of Web 2.0 and the rising accessibility of social media platforms.

Individuals may promote their abilities, experience, and lifestyles on social media sites such as Instagram, YouTube, TikTok, and Twitter. Influencers have emerged as major people with large followings and strong influence over their audiences. They've developed personal brands and communities around their content, which ranges from beauty and fashion to fitness, travel, and cuisine.

Influencers are distinguished by their ability to engage with their followers on a personal level. Influencers, unlike traditional celebrities, are frequently perceived as personable and approachable. They interact with their audience through honest and often uncensored material, revealing peeks into their everyday lives, offering advice, and developing trusting and authentic connections.

Social media influencers' effect extends beyond just entertainment or inspiration. Their suggestions, product ratings, and endorsements have a strong influence on customer behavior. Followers regard influencers as reliable sources of information and seek their advice when making purchase decisions. As a result, influencer marketing has grown in popularity, in which corporations collaborate with influencers to promote their products or services to a highly engaged and focused audience.

Influencers have used their internet presence to develop profitable careers. They make money through a variety of means, including as brand collaborations, sponsored content, affiliate marketing, and the development of their own products or services. Because of the financial possibilities, many people have chosen to work as social media influencers, creating a highly competitive field.

While the rise of social media influencers has created tremendous benefits, it has also created significant obstacles. Influencers are under pressure to provide interesting and high-quality material on a continuous basis, maintain their online reputation, and stay relevant in a fast-paced digital world. They are also responsible for utilizing their influence responsibly and publicly, revealing brand partnerships, and retaining their audience's confidence.

Social media influencers have also had a huge impact on popular culture. They have reshaped aesthetic standards, launched trends, and increased the visibility of social problems. Their reach goes beyond the internet arena, as they frequently cooperate with businesses, feature in conventional media, and become sought-after individuals in a variety of sectors.

The growth of social media influencers signifies a shift in how people achieve popularity and wield power. It emphasizes the digital age's importance of honest narrative, personal branding, and community interaction. As social media evolves, so will influencers' roles and effect, affecting how we consume information, make purchase decisions, and interact with online platforms.

Defining Your Influencer Niche

Identifying your influencer niche is an important first step in becoming a great social media influencer. It entails focusing on a certain area of knowledge or interest in which you may position yourself as an authority and connect with a specialized audience.

Consider your hobbies, talents, knowledge, and unique viewpoint while defining your influencer niche. What issues are you passionate about? What do you actually care about? What areas of knowledge or experiences do you have that you can share with others?

Begin by brainstorming several prospective niches that correspond to your hobbies and experience. Consider fashion, cosmetics, fitness, travel, parenthood, technology, or any other topic that interests you. Consider which components of these categories you may specialize in, since restricting your emphasis can help you stand out in a congested digital market.

Once you've identified a few viable niches, undertake market research to determine demand and competition in each one. Examine the content, audience engagement, and development of influencers who are already successful in those areas. This study will give you information about the possible audience size, engagement opportunities, and areas where you can contribute a distinct viewpoint.

Next, assess your personal skills and distinguishing characteristics that will set you apart in your selected sector. Identify your own brand traits, such as narrative style, personality, or knowledge, that can assist you in connecting authentically with your target audience.

Consider the demographics of your target audience, as well as their hobbies and problem issues. Who do you want to reach out to with your content? What are their preferences, requirements, and difficulties? Understanding your audience will allow you to personalize your content and messaging to their needs and establish a devoted following.

Once you've found your influencer niche, you must continuously publish content that is relevant to it. Create a content strategy that focuses on delivering value, solving issues, or motivating your specific audience. This will assist you in establishing yourself as a credible source of information in your neighborhood.

Remember that your influencer niche is fluid and might change over time. You may discover possibilities to enhance or expand your specialization as you acquire experience and feedback from your audience. It is critical to be adaptable and responsive to your audience's shifting interests and demands.

Identifying your influencer niche is an important first step in your journey as a social media influencer. It enables you to develop your expertise, connect with a specific audience, and set yourself out from the competitors. You can establish yourself as a go-to authority in your area by continuously generating good content and building a strong and engaged community around your brand.

Identifying your influencer niche is an important first step in becoming a great social media influencer. It entails choosing and narrowing down the exact region or issue on which you will concentrate your material and expertise. This method is critical because it allows you to build a distinct personality, attract a specific audience, and distinguish yourself from other influencers.

Begin by researching your own hobbies, interests, and areas of experience to identify your influencer niche. Consider the topics that actually interest you, as well as the information or talents you have that may help others. Consider your own point of view or experiences that can set you apart from the pack in the congested social media scene.

Make a list of prospective niches that correspond to your hobbies and experience. It might be fashion, beauty, fitness, travel, cuisine, parenthood, technology, or any other area that interests you. Try to uncover distinct sub-niches or specialized regions inside these bigger niches that you may carve out as your own.

Conduct extensive market research to assess demand and competition in each prospective area. Investigate successful influencers in certain fields to learn about their content, audience engagement, and development. Analyze their strengths and shortcomings, discover gaps or neglected sectors, and look for possibilities to contribute a fresh viewpoint or approach.

As you narrow down your options, consider your individual talents and attributes that will set you apart in your selected sector. Consider your narrative style, attitude, skill, or any other unique aspect you may present to your audience to provide value. These distinguishing features can assist you in developing your unique brand and creating a real relationship with your audience.

Understanding your target audience is also critical. Define the demographics, interests, and demands of the target audience. Determine their pain issues, desires, and preferences in order to adapt your content and marketing to them individually. This tailored strategy will assist you in developing a loyal network of followers that are interested in your area and find value in your material.

Once you've identified your influencer niche, create a content plan centered on that issue. Create a steady stream of material that is relevant to your niche and connects with your readers. Provide instructive, amusing, or inspirational material that speaks to their needs and interests in your area of expertise. This will position you as a credible authority and go-to resource for your target audience.

Remember that creating your influencer niche is not a one-time event. You may discover possibilities to enhance or expand your specialization as you acquire experience, feedback, and insights from your audience. Accept the freedom to adapt and evolve your niche while being true to your basic principles and interests.

To summarize, choosing your influencer niche is critical for building your brand, engaging a specific audience, and standing out in the competitive social media market. You may position yourself as an authority, gain credibility, and cultivate a dedicated community of followers who engage with and appreciate your work by carefully picking and focusing in on a certain subject.

Chapter 2: Crafting Your Personal Brand

Identifying Your Unique Value Proposition

Identifying your unique value proposition is a critical step in developing a successful personal brand and becoming an influential social media user. It entails comprehending and communicating the particular value that you provide to your audience, which distinguishes you from other influencers in your industry.

Your unique value proposition (UVP) is the mix of your talents, knowledge, personality, and point of view that distinguishes you and makes you desirable to your target audience. It provides a solution to the question, "Why should someone follow and engage with you over other influencers?"

Begin by considering your skills, hobbies, and areas of competence to determine your UVP. Consider what distinguishes you from others in your field. What special abilities, expertise, or experiences do you have that will benefit and resonate with your audience? Consider the unique difficulties or requirements you can solve, the insights you can provide, and the inspiration you can supply.

Consider your individuality and true voice as well. How can you engage and connect with your audience in a true and approachable manner? What distinguishing features and attributes distinguish you? Embrace your uniqueness and the characteristics of your personality that will appeal to your target audience.

Conduct a comprehensive examination of your niche's rivals and influencers. Determine what they provide and how they present themselves. This study can help you grasp the market's gaps and possibilities, allowing you to carve out your own distinct niche.

Engage your current audience or do research to learn about their wants, desires, and pain areas. Understanding your audience's difficulties and goals will allow you to adapt your UVP to meet their demands. It is critical to match your particular assets and expertise to the desires and demands of your target audience.

Create a captivating statement that concisely and effectively expresses your UVP. This statement should emphasize the main advantages, solutions, or experiences that you provide to your target audience. It should explain why your target audience should pick you as their go-to influencer in your field.

Make sure your material regularly represents and reinforces your UVP. Create content that reflects your unique abilities and ideals, and give value and authenticity to your audience on a constant basis. This will strengthen your reputation and set you apart from other influencers.

Evaluate and adjust your UVP on a regular basis as your personal brand changes and your audience's demands change. Keep an eye on your audience's input and adjust your UVP as needed to ensure its continued relevance and efficacy.

Identifying your unique value proposition (UVP) is a critical step in developing a successful personal brand and becoming an influential social media user. Your unique value proposition (UVP) is what distinguishes you from others in your area and expresses the particular value you deliver to your audience.

Begin by thinking on your skills, interests, and areas of competence to identify your UVP. Consider what makes you special and sets you apart from other influencers. Consider the special talents, expertise, or experiences you have that can help your audience. Understanding your distinct characteristics allows you to determine what makes you valued and exceptional.

Consider your personality as well as your natural voice. Consider how you may interact and connect with your audience in a true and relatable way. Accept your uniqueness and let your personality show through. Your distinguishing features and characteristics can help you stand out and appeal to your target audience.

Conduct a thorough examination of your niche's rivals and influencers. Recognize what they provide and how they position themselves. This study can assist you in identifying market gaps and opportunities that you may use to differentiate yourself. Look for places where you can provide a different viewpoint or something that others may not.

Engage your current audience and undertake research to learn about their wants, desires, and pain areas. You may successfully meet your audience's individual requirements by knowing their issues and objectives. To establish a solid connection, align your unique assets and expertise with the goals and requirements of your target audience.

Create a convincing statement that expresses your UVP effectively. This statement should emphasize the main advantages, solutions, or experiences that you provide to your target audience. It should encapsulate what makes you unique and resonate with your target audience. Keep it short, to the point, and simple to grasp.

Make sure your material regularly represents and reinforces your UVP. Create material that reflects your distinct qualities, values, and expertise. Deliver value and authenticity to your audience on a consistent basis, reinforcing your UVP with each piece of content you publish. This consistency will strengthen your reputation and distinguish you from the competition.

Evaluate and adjust your UVP on a regular basis as your personal brand changes and your audience's demands change. Keep an open mind and alter your UVP to stay current and appealing. Maintain your competitive advantage by keeping an eye on the shifting landscape of your specialty and adjusting your UVP accordingly.

You can distinguish yourself from other influencers and build a compelling personal brand by recognizing and using your unique value offer. Your unique value proposition (UVP) will attract and resonate with your target audience, encourage loyalty, and position you as a trusted and prominent figure in your area.

Developing Your Authentic Voice

Being a great social media influencer requires you to develop your authentic voice. Your true voice is the distinct manner in which you express yourself and interact with your audience, expressing your personality, beliefs, and point of view. It is critical in developing trust, connection, and engagement with your followers.

Begin by accepting your own self in order to build your unique voice. Instead than attempting to emulate or replicate someone else's style, be authentic and loyal to yourself. Determine your essential values, beliefs, and interests. Recognize what is important to you and what you stand for. Your true voice is built on this self-awareness.

Expressing vulnerability may also help you build your real voice. Tell your readers about your real-life experiences, problems, and personal tales. You establish a sense of relatability and empathy by opening up, which enhances your relationship with your fans. Showcasing your true self allows you to stand out in a sea of influencers.

In order to build your true voice, you must be consistent. Maintain a consistent tone and messaging across your material while being loyal to your principles. Consistency fosters trust and assists your audience in recognizing and responding to your distinct voice. It also creates a sense of authenticity since your followers can count on you to be constant in what you provide.

Actively listen and respond to your audience. Take note of their remarks, questions, and feedback. Genuine dialogues and genuine interest in your audience serve to establish a feeling of community and build trust. You may better address your audience's needs and improve your true relationship with them by actively listening.

Experiment with various content forms and styles to discover what feels natural and comfortable to you. It may take some trial and error to find the ideal technique to convey your true self. Don't be hesitant to experiment with fresh innovative ways. As you acquire experience and find your rhythm, your distinct perspective and style will emerge.

Remember that being honest does not imply being flawless or attempting to please everyone. It's about being yourself and expressing your authentic views, opinions, and experiences. Accept your oddities, flaws, and distinct personality features. Your audience will respect your honesty and will connect with you on a deeper level as a result.

Finally, be loyal to your ideals and resist the temptation to sacrifice your authenticity for the sake of popularity or trends. Authenticity is what distinguishes you and draws a devoted and interested audience. It's preferable to have a small but engaged audience that connects with your real voice over a huge following that doesn't connect with who you truly are.

Continuing on the theme of creating your genuine voice, keep in mind that authenticity is not just about what you say, but also about how you express it. Take note of the language, tone, and style you employ in your article. Maintain a conversational and relevant tone that is appealing to your readers.

Being truthful and honest with your audience is also part of being authentic. Share your creative process, behind-the-scenes experiences, and even problems you face. Transparency develops trust and a closer relationship with your followers, who value your genuineness and transparency.

Avoid the desire to emulate or mimic others. While it's natural to be inspired by other influencers, it's critical to create your own voice and style. Accept your uniqueness and contribute your own point of view to the table. Your authenticity comes from being genuine to oneself and bringing something unique to the digital arena.

In order to build your true voice, you must be consistent. Keep a steady presence and frequency of information distribution in mind. This not only helps you establish a trustworthy reputation, but it also strengthens your voice and message. Your audience will grow to anticipate and value your continuous portrayal of your true self.

Seek input from your audience as you create your real voice. Engage in dialogues, solicit their feedback, and consider their recommendations. Feedback may provide useful information about how your audience views your content and voice. Use this constructive comments to improve and enhance your true voice over time.

Take chances and explore new creative areas without fear. Experiment with various sorts of material, new forms, and emerging trends. Be open to change and progress while being loyal to your actual self. As you study new topics or engage with other people within your specialization, your unique voice may develop.

Remember that authenticity is a continuous journey. Maintain awareness of your own personal growth and changes, and allow your real voice to evolve naturally. Make an effort to connect with your audience on a personal level, and always emphasize being true to yourself and your ideals.

Finally, building your own voice as a social media influencer is an ongoing process. It entails being consistent, open, and relatable while embracing your actual self. Maintain an open mind to input, take reasonable chances, and let your voice grow naturally. You will make a deep connection with your audience, gain trust, and leave a lasting impression as an influencer if you cultivate your true voice.

Building an Engaging Online Persona

Creating an appealing online identity is essential for being a successful social media influencer. Your online persona is the picture you display to your audience, which includes your personality, style, and interactions with others. You can acquire and sustain a dedicated and engaged following by creating a compelling online presence.

Begin by outlining the primary features and attributes you wish to project in your online presence. Consider how you want your audience to see you and the image you want to project. Choose a tone and style that complements your content and connects with your intended audience. Consistency in your demeanor, whether kind, hilarious, inspirational, or educational, aids in the creation of an identifiable and relevant personality.

Developing your online identity requires authenticity. Be authentic and let your personality reflect through your articles. Showcasing your actual self allows you to connect with your audience on a deeper level because they can relate to and identify with your genuine expression. Avoid attempting to be someone you are not, since your audience will enjoy and interact with your actual self more.

Building a compelling online persona requires engagement. Respond to comments, messages, and engage in conversations to actively communicate with your audience. Demonstrate genuine interest in and gratitude for their assistance and feedback. You may establish a devoted and enthusiastic fan following by cultivating a feeling of community and regularly connecting with your fans.

Consistency is essential in developing a compelling online character. Maintain a consistent publishing schedule and make sure your material is relevant to your persona. Consistency informs your audience about what to anticipate from you and fosters trust. It also helps you to establish a recognized style and polish your identity over time.

Storytelling is an effective method for developing a compelling online character. Create captivating stories that attract and resonate with your audience. To establish an emotional connection, share personal experiences, problems, and accomplishments. Improve your storytelling abilities by weaving storylines into your material and making your viewers feel as though they are a part of your trip.

Visual aesthetics are important in developing a compelling online identity. Use consistent colors, typefaces, and graphics in your material to create a unified and aesthetically attractive brand. Visual coherence aids in the creation of a recognised and professional image. Take care of the quality of your photographs and videos because they contribute to the overall appeal of your online presence.

Building a compelling online image also requires flexibility and adaptation. Keep up with trends, listen to input from your audience, and adjust your character accordingly. Accept new platforms, features, or content formats that are consistent with your brand and enable you to interact with your audience in novel ways.

Creating an appealing online presence is an important step toward being a great social media influencer. Your online persona is the digital version of yourself that you portray to your audience, and it is crucial in attracting and maintaining followers.

Begin by establishing the primary features and attributes you wish to represent while creating a compelling online presence. Think about the image and personality you want to convey. Consider how you want your audience to see you and the type of material you want to provide. Do you want to be perceived as informed and authoritative, personable and approachable, or entertaining and humorous? Defining these characteristics aids in the creation of a clear and consistent image that connects with your target audience.

When developing your online presence, authenticity is essential. Be authentic and let your personality reflect through your articles. Avoid attempting to replicate or emulate others, since your own voice and viewpoint are what set you apart. Accept your uniqueness and express your genuine thoughts, experiences, and opinions. Your authentic self will be appreciated and connected with by your audience.

Building a compelling online persona necessitates engagement. Respond to comments, messages, and engage in conversations to actively communicate with your audience. Ask questions, solicit opinion, and value your followers' response to demonstrate genuine interest in them. Creating a feeling of community and encouraging two-way dialogue strengthens your relationship with your audience, keeping them interested and invested in your content.

Building a compelling online persona requires consistency. Maintain a consistent publishing schedule and make sure your material is relevant to your persona. Consistency helps your audience create expectations and fosters trust. Maintaining consistency, whether in the tone of your writing, the style of your images, or the frequency of your updates, helps consolidate your online presence and builds a recognizable brand image.

Storytelling is an effective method for developing a compelling online character. Create fascinating storylines that will fascinate and move your audience. Share personal tales, anecdotes, or motivational stories with your audience. Effective storytelling helps you connect with your audience on a deeper level and keeps them coming back for more.

Visual appeal is equally important in developing a compelling online identity. Pay attention to the visual parts of your material, such as photo quality, video composition, and the overall style of your feed or profile. Consistent and aesthetically attractive information contributes to the creation of a unified and professional picture that improves your online presence.

As an influencer, it is critical to foster flexibility and adaptability. Maintain an open mind to new trends, platforms, and content formats that complement your brand and resonate with your target audience. Accept change and be open to experiment and adapt your online presence as needed to stay current and satisfy your audience's changing requirements and preferences.

Finally, developing an appealing online presence includes establishing your intended image, embracing authenticity, encouraging participation, keeping consistency, leveraging narrative, paying attention to visual aesthetics, and being adaptive. You can make a deep connection with your audience, establish yourself as a trusted influencer, and leave a lasting impression in the digital sphere by carefully building and cultivating your online image.

Chapter 3: Choosing the Right Platforms

Evaluating Different Social Media Platforms

Evaluating various social media sites is an important step in establishing your influencer social media strategy. Each platform has its own set of features, demographics, and interaction dynamics, making it critical to determine which platforms are most suited to your objectives and target audience.

Begin by becoming familiar with the major social media networks. Instagram, YouTube, Facebook, Twitter, TikTok, LinkedIn, and Pinterest each have their own set of advantages and user demographics. Investigate and become acquainted with the platforms to acquire insights into their user population, content formats, interaction patterns, and the sorts of influencers that flourish on each.

Take into account your target audience's preferences. Determine the demographics, interests, and habits of your prospective audience. Determine which platforms are most popular with your target audience and provide the most effective way of reaching out to and connecting with them. If your target audience is predominantly youthful, visually-oriented people, sites like Instagram or TikTok may be more appropriate.

Examine the content types and formats that each platform supports. Examine whether platforms are compatible with your content strategy and the sort of material you intend to produce. Platforms like Instagram or YouTube, for example, may be a good fit if you are great at making aesthetically attractive photographs or videos. Platforms like Twitter may be more ideal if you enjoy text-based material or engaging in real-time conversations.

Consider the options for participation and interaction afforded by each platform. On each channel, assess the degree of involvement and interaction you can have with your audience. Some platforms provide tools such as comments, direct messaging, live streaming, and community groups that can help you engage with your audience. Examine how well these characteristics match your communication style and engagement goals.

Examine each platform's monetization prospects and influencer marketing options. Investigate how influencers on each network might earn money via brand collaborations, sponsored content, or advertising. On each platform, assess the potential for development and the amount of competition in your area. Consider the long-term feasibility and profitability of participating on a certain platform.

Determine the amount of time and resources needed to maintain an active presence on each platform. Each platform has its own standards for content production, publishing, and interaction. To assess if you can regularly offer high-quality content on a certain platform, consider your available time, resources, and content development capabilities. Focusing on a few platforms and excelling at them is preferable than spreading oneself too thin over several channels.

Finally, perform a competitive study of influencers in your field across several channels. Examine the success and levels of engagement of influencers who post comparable material and reach a similar audience. Analyze their techniques on various platforms and estimate your chances of standing out and thriving in that competitive landscape.

Evaluating various social media platforms is an important step for influencers who want to build a strong online presence. With so many platforms accessible, each with its own set of features and user demographics, it's critical to carefully consider which platforms are the greatest fit for your objectives and target audience.

Begin by learning everything you can about the major social media networks. Instagram, YouTube, Facebook, Twitter, TikTok, LinkedIn, and Pinterest each have their own individual features, user bases, and content types. Take the time to investigate and become acquainted with these platforms, learning about their functions, user demographics, interaction patterns, and the sorts of influencers that flourish on each.

Take into account your target audience's preferences. Determine your desired audience's demographic characteristics, interests, and habits. This understanding can assist you in determining which platforms are most popular among your target audience and provide the most effective way of reaching and connecting with them. For example, if your target audience includes mostly of young, visually-oriented people, sites such as Instagram or TikTok may be the best alternatives.

Examine the content types and formats that each platform supports. Examine how effectively each platform fits into your content strategy and the sort of material you intend to produce. For example, if you excel in creating aesthetically attractive photographs or films, sites like Instagram or YouTube may be an excellent place to showcase your skills. Platforms like Twitter, on the other hand, may be more ideal for your requirements if you enjoy text-based information or engaging in real-time chats.

Consider the options for participation and interaction afforded by each platform. Examine the degree of involvement and engagement you can have with your audience on each site. Some platforms provide tools like comments, direct messaging, live streaming, and community groups that may help you engage with and respond to your audience. Examine how effectively these elements mesh with your communication style and engagement objectives.

Examine each platform's monetization prospects and influencer marketing options. Investigate how influencers on each network might earn money via brand collaborations, sponsored content, or advertising. On each platform, assess the potential for development and the amount of competition in your area. Consider the long-term feasibility and profitability of participating on a certain platform.

Determine the amount of time and resources needed to maintain an active presence on each platform. Each platform has its own standards for content production, publishing, and interaction. To assess if you can regularly offer high-quality content on a certain platform, consider your available time, resources, and content development capabilities. Focusing on a few platforms and excelling at them is preferable than spreading oneself too thin over several channels.

Finally, perform a competitive study of influencers in your field across several channels. Examine the success and levels of engagement of influencers who post comparable material and reach a similar audience. Analyze their techniques on various platforms and estimate your chances of standing out and thriving in that competitive landscape.

You may make educated judgments about where to focus your time and energy as an influencer by carefully assessing different social media sites. Choose the platforms that best fit your objectives, target audience, content strategy, engagement opportunities, and revenue potential. Remember that platforms vary over time, so examine your platform selections on a regular basis to ensure they still correspond with your growth and audience goals.

Selecting Your Primary Platforms

For influencers, deciding on your key platforms is critical since it dictates where you will focus your efforts and devote your time and money. You may choose the platforms that will best support your development and success by carefully analyzing your goals, target audience, content strategy, and interaction preferences.

Begin by defining your objectives as an influencer. What do you want to accomplish with your web presence? Understanding your objectives can assist drive your platform decision process, whether it's establishing a devoted community, expanding brand collaborations, or driving visitors to your website.

Consider your target audience's chosen platforms next. Determine the demographics, interests, and habits of your target audience. Investigate which platforms are most popular with your target demographic and provide the most prospects for interaction and reach. You can enhance the effect of your content and connect with the appropriate people by concentrating on the platforms your audience uses.

Examine your content strategy and the kinds of material you want to produce. Images, videos, articles, and live streaming are all supported by different platforms. Align your content strategy with platforms that best display your skills and enable you to successfully communicate your message. Platforms like

Instagram or YouTube, for example, may be great if you specialize at making aesthetically engaging material.

Take into account your involvement preferences and communication style. Some systems include additional participatory elements like comments, direct messages, or live video. Platforms like Twitter or live streaming platforms may be a fantastic choice if you thrive on real-time dialogues and direct connection with your audience. To develop genuine connections with your audience, use platforms that correspond with your preferred ways of engagement.

Analyze each platform's monetization prospects and influencer marketing opportunities. Investigate how influencers create cash on various platforms, such as brand collaborations, sponsored content, or advertising. Consider the market competitiveness and development potential of your specialty on each platform. Determine the long-term profitability and viability of participating on a specific platform.

Consider how much time and money you have to devote to maintaining an active presence on each network. To develop and distribute content, connect with your audience, and remain up to speed on platform-specific trends and features, each platform necessitates time and effort. Evaluate your capacity and bandwidth to offer high-quality content on each platform on a constant basis. Focusing on a few platforms and excelling at them is preferable than spreading oneself too thin over several channels.

Finally, consider the possibility of cross-platform promotion and integration. Choose platforms that make cross-promotion and integration of your content simple. This allows you to use your presence on one platform to generate traffic and interaction on others, so increasing your total reach and effect.

Influencers must choose their key platforms carefully in order to efficiently utilize their time and resources. To choose the platforms that will best support your development and success, assess your goals, target audience, content strategy, interaction preferences, monetization possibilities, and available resources.

Begin by outlining your objectives as an influencer. Determine your objectives for your internet presence. Having defined objectives can drive your platform selection approach, whether it's growing a committed community, generating brand collaborations, boosting website traffic, or demonstrating your skills.

Next, investigate your target audience's favorite platforms. Understand the demographics, interests, and habits of your target audience. Investigate which platforms have the best potential for interaction and reach with your target audience. You may enhance the effect of your content and connect with the appropriate people by concentrating on platforms that your audience actively utilizes.

Examine your content strategy and the kinds of material you want to produce. Different platforms support different types of material, such as photographs, videos, articles, and live streaming. Align your content strategy with platforms that best display your skills and enable you to successfully communicate your message. If you excel in creating aesthetically appealing material, for example, sites like Instagram or YouTube may be great for showcasing your abilities.

Take into account your involvement preferences and communication style. Some systems include additional participatory elements like comments, direct messages, or live video. Platforms like Twitter or live streaming platforms may be well-suited to your needs if you thrive on real-time dialogues and direct connection with your audience. To develop genuine connections with your audience, use platforms that correspond with your preferred ways of engagement.

Analyze each platform's monetization prospects and influencer marketing opportunities. Investigate how influencers make money on various platforms, such as through brand collaborations, sponsored content, or advertising. Take into account the market competitiveness and development potential of your specialty on each platform. Examine the long-term profitability and feasibility of being active on a certain platform, taking into account the possibility for partnerships and monetization options.

Consider how much time and resources you have to devote to maintaining an active presence on each network. To produce and distribute content, connect with your audience, and remain up to speed on platform-specific trends and features, each platform necessitates significant time and effort. Evaluate your capability and availability to offer high-quality content on each platform on a continuous basis. Focusing on a few platforms and excelling at them is frequently preferable than spreading oneself too thin over several channels.

Finally, think about the possibility of cross-platform promotion and integration. Choose platforms that enable for smooth cross-promotion and content integration. This allows you to use your presence on one platform to generate traffic and interaction on others, so increasing your total reach and effect.

You may optimize your efforts as an influencer and maximize your effect by carefully picking your major channels. Select platforms that are compatible with your objectives, target audience, content strategy, engagement preferences, and revenue possibilities. Reevaluate your platform selections on a regular basis to ensure they continue to support your development and correspond with the changing demands and preferences of your audience.

Exploring Supplementary Platforms

Exploring other channels is a critical step for influencers looking to increase their online presence and reach a larger audience.

While major platforms form the backbone of your social media strategy, supplemental platforms provide extra options to engage with other user populations and vary your content distribution.

Begin your exploration of supplemental platforms by finding platforms that correspond to your target audience and content strategy. Consider your target audience's demographics, interests, and behaviors. Investigate platforms with overlapping user bases with your target demographic but that may provide a distinct value proposition or content style in comparison to your core platforms.

Examine the content formats and functionalities that each supplemental platform supports. Look for platforms that let you present your material in novel and entertaining ways. Consider networks like Pinterest or Snapchat, which thrive in visual storytelling, if you primarily rely on visual content. If your material is more educational or professional in nature, networks such as LinkedIn or Medium may allow you to reach a distinct target niche.

Consider the potential for participation and interaction afforded by each extra platform. Examine the platform's features that allow you to communicate with your audience in meaningful ways, such as comments, messaging, or community groups. Look for platforms that encourage two-way conversation and develop a sense of community, allowing you to connect with others and position yourself as an authority in your field.

Examine the scalability and growth potential of each supplemental platform. Examine the platform's user base and growth trajectory to see if it fits your long-term objectives. Look for platforms that are increasing and have a growing audience, since they might give opportunity to broaden your reach and impact.

Determine the time and resources needed to maintain an active presence on each additional platform. Consider the increased workload and content generation requirements that come with moving to new platforms. Examine your ability to offer high-quality material and communicate with your audience across numerous channels without jeopardizing the quality of your major platforms.

Investigate the cross-promotion and integration possibilities between your primary and secondary platforms. Consider how you may use your existing content and audience to drive traffic and interaction to your supplemental channels. You may increase your total reach and build a unified online presence by effectively integrating your presence across platforms.

Evaluate the performance and effect of your additional platforms on a regular basis. Monitor engagement data, audience growth, and audience feedback to see whether the extra channels are producing the expected effects. Adjust your approach and resource allocation depending on the platforms that produce the highest results and correspond with your overall aims.

Exploring other channels is an effective method for influencers looking to expand their online presence and interact with a larger audience. While primary platforms are the foundation of your social media strategy, secondary platforms provide extra chances to reach different demographics, diversify content types, and broaden your total effect.

To successfully investigate supplemental platforms, begin by selecting platforms that correspond with your target audience and content strategy. Consider your target audience's demographics, interests, and behaviors. Look for platforms with a user base that coincides with your target demographic but that provide different features or content formats than your major platforms.

Examine the content formats and functionalities that each supplemental platform supports. Consider how well the platform enables you to present your material in compelling and novel ways. For example, if visual material is your major focus, networks such as Pinterest or Instagram Reels may provide extra options for visual storytelling. If your material is more educational or professional in nature, networks such as LinkedIn or Medium may offer opportunities to distribute long-form pieces or industry insights.

Consider the potential for participation and interaction afforded by each extra platform. Examine the platform's features, including as comments, messaging, and community groups, to see how they might help you engage with your audience on a deeper level. Look for platforms that promote meaningful connections and a feeling of community, allowing you to create relationships and position yourself as an authority in your field.

Examine the scalability and growth possibilities of each additional platform. Investigate the platform's user base, growth trajectory, and trends to see if they correspond with your long-term objectives. Look for platforms that are growing and have an active community, since these can give possibilities to broaden your reach and impact over time.

Determine the time and resources needed to maintain an active presence on each additional platform. Consider the increased workload and content generation requirements that come with moving to new platforms. Examine your ability to offer high-quality material and communicate with your audience across numerous channels without jeopardizing the quality of your major platforms. It's critical to establish a balance and avoid being too spread out over too many platforms.

Investigate the possibility of cross-promotion and integration between your principal and secondary platforms. Consider how you may use your existing content and audience to drive traffic and interaction to your supplemental channels. To encourage your audience to investigate and follow you on your auxiliary media, share teasers or bits of material from those sites on your major networks.

Evaluate the performance and effect of your additional platforms on a regular basis. Monitor engagement data, audience growth, and audience feedback to see whether the extra channels are producing the expected effects. Adjust your strategy and resource allocation based on this research to focus on the platforms that generate the highest returns and correspond with your overall aims.

Finally, experimenting with new platforms helps influencers to broaden their online presence and reach new audiences and content types. You may expand your reach, interact with new communities, and exploit the unique features and possibilities given by each platform by choosing platforms that correspond with your target demographic, content strategy, and engagement preferences. Assess the performance of your supplemental platforms on a regular basis and adjust your plan as needed to ensure they contribute to your overall development and success as an influencer.

Chapter 4: Creating Compelling Content
Understanding Content Types and Formats

Understanding different types of content and formats is critical for influencers who want to generate interesting and powerful material for their audience. The overall categories or topics of the material you generate are referred to as content types, whereas formats are the precise methods you display and deliver that content to your audience.

Depending on your niche and target audience, content genres might differ greatly. They can include, among other things, instructional information, entertainment content, inspiring content, product reviews, tutorials, behind-the-scenes peeks, personal tales, or industry insights. Understanding the major content kinds that engage with your audience and align with your skills and interests is critical.

Once you've determined your content kinds, you may experiment with different formats to efficiently show and convey your material. Formats are the many channels and ways through which you deliver your message. Some examples of common content formats are:

Articles, blog entries, captions, and written social media updates are examples of written content. Through well-crafted written tales, you may convey specific information, communicate views and opinions, and engage your audience.

Images, infographics, drawings, or graphics are examples of visual content. It aids in the transmission of information, the evocation of emotions, and the capture of attention. Platforms such as Instagram and Pinterest are ideal for visual content makers.

Video Content: Videos are extremely entertaining and adaptable. They might be brief or long, and they can take many different formats, such as vlogs, tutorials, interviews, or product reviews. For video content providers, platforms such as YouTube, TikTok, and Instagram Reels are popular.

Podcasts, audio recordings, and voiceovers are examples of audio content forms. They enable you to share tales, thoughts, or engage in dialogue with your audience. For audio material dissemination, platforms such as Spotify and Apple Podcasts are often employed.

Live Content: Live streaming services such as Instagram Live, Facebook Live, and YouTube Live allow you to communicate with your audience in real time. This style enables for quick interaction, Q&A sessions, and behind-the-scenes peeks.

The use of interactive content fosters audience participation and engagement. Polls, quizzes, sweepstakes, and interactive tales are some examples. Interactive content may be utilized on platforms such as Instagram and Facebook, as well as through third-party technologies such as website plugins.

Infographics and data visualizations offer complicated information or data in a visually appealing and readily accessible style. They can be used as single photos or as part of longer-form material.

Consider your audience's preferences, platform capabilities, and your personal talents and interests when choosing content kinds and formats. Experiment with several forms to see which ones resonate most with your audience and allow you to successfully express your message. Remember to stick to your selected formats in order to retain a consistent brand image and engage your audience over time.

Finally, knowing content kinds and formats enables you to develop diverse and interesting content that caters to the tastes of your audience while effectively communicating your message. You may engage your audience, demonstrate your expertise, and develop a devoted following as an influencer by including a variety of content kinds and formats into your plan.

Mastering the Art of Storytelling

Mastering the art of storytelling allows influencers to engage their audience, develop emotional connections, and successfully communicate their message. Storytelling is more than just presenting information; it is about creating narratives that connect with your audience and make an impression. Influencers may engage their audience, motivate action, and develop a distinctive brand presence by mastering the main principles of storytelling.

Begin by determining the goal of your tale. Determine if you aim to amuse, educate, inspire, or provoke emotions with your narrative. Clarifying your storytelling goals can help you steer the development of your tale and connect with your audience on a deeper level.

Create a good story framework. A well-crafted tale will generally include an introduction, a growing action, a climax, and a resolution. As the tale continues, introduce the key characters, create the setting, and build anticipation. The climax should be the height of excitement or suspense, while the resolution provides closure and conveys the story's message or moral.

Create characters that are relatable. Characters serve as the foundation of your tale and should be relevant to your audience. Create characters who represent qualities, difficulties, or experiences that your audience can relate to. This helps your viewers to identify with the characters and develop an emotional connection with them.

Incorporate conflict and emotions. Emotions are a strong narrative tool. Through your story, elicit emotions such as joy, empathy, surprise, or inspiration. Create suspense and keep your audience involved by introducing conflict or difficulties that the characters must overcome.

Use rich imagery and sensory details. Using descriptive language and sensory information, create a vivid image in the minds of your audience. Engage their senses by appealing to their vision, hearing, taste, touch, and smell. This contributes to a more immersive experience, which makes your tale more memorable and compelling.

Use narrative tactics like foreshadowing, suspense, and plot twists. These tactics keep your audience interested and waiting to see what occurs next. To surprise and fascinate your audience, use foreshadowing to hint at future events, develop tension by progressively exposing information, or provide unexpected story twists.

Incorporate sincerity and vulnerability into your narratives. To establish a true connection with your audience, share personal tales, experiences, or obstacles. Authenticity encourages trust and relatability, allowing your audience to see the genuine person behind the material and build a stronger link.

Create a captivating beginning and a memorable finale. Capture your audience's interest right away with a unique opener that draws them in. The conclusion should make an impact and support the idea or takeaway that you wish to express. It might be a strong quotation, a thought-provoking question, or a call to action that inspires your audience to think or act.

Practice narrative elements including timing, tone, and delivery. To create a dynamic narrative, vary the speed of your story, choosing slower times for introspection and anticipation and quicker ones for thrill. To fit the atmosphere and emotions of your tale, adjust your tone. Take care with your delivery, whether it's written text, video, or audio, to ensure it adds to the narrative experience.

Finally, examine your audience's comments and involvement. Monitor the reaction to your tales and solicit feedback to see what connects with your target audience. Based on this input, adapt and enhance your storytelling strategies to consistently increase your capacity to engage and connect with your audience.

Mastering the art of storytelling is a must for influencers who want to capture their audience and leave a lasting impression. Storytelling is more than just passing on information; it is weaving narratives that connect with your audience, elicit emotions, and successfully deliver your message. You can captivate your audience, motivate action, and develop a distinctive brand presence by knowing the main principles of storytelling and refining your storytelling talents.

To begin, you must determine the goal of your tale. Determine your goals for storytelling, whether they be to amuse, educate, inspire, or evoke emotions. Clarifying your storytelling goals can help you steer the development of your tale and connect with your audience on a deeper level.

Effective storytelling requires a solid narrative framework. Make a well-structured tale with an introduction, escalating action, climax, and resolution. Introduce the key characters, create the setting, and generate suspense as the tale progresses. The climax should be the height of excitement, suspense, or transformation, while the resolution provides closure and conveys the story's major message or moral.

Create characters that are both relatable and interesting. Characters are at the center of your tale, acting as a link between the audience and the narrative. Create characters who represent qualities, difficulties, or experiences that your audience can relate to. This helps your viewers to emotionally connect with the characters and emotionally invest in the plot.

In order to engage your audience, use emotions and conflict. Emotions are a strong narrative tool. Through your story, elicit emotions such as joy, empathy, surprise, or inspiration. Create suspense and keep your audience engrossed in the conclusion by introducing conflict or difficulties that the characters must overcome.

Use vivid descriptions and sensory elements to create a mental image for your viewers. Engage their senses by appealing to their vision, hearing, taste, touch, and smell. Descriptive language and sensory elements offer a more immersive experience, bringing your tale to life and leaving your audience with a lasting impression.

To enhance interest and fascinate your audience, use narrative tactics such as foreshadowing, suspense, or plot twists. To generate anticipation, foreshadow future events, develop tension by progressively exposing information, or surprise and interest your audience with unexpected story twists.

Authenticity and vulnerability are essential for connecting with your audience. Share personal tales, experiences, or obstacles that relate to your story's major topic. You urge your audience to relate to your experiences and build a stronger bond by opening up and exhibiting vulnerability.

Create a captivating beginning and a memorable finale. Begin by capturing your audience's attention with an engaging opener that piques their curiosity or stimulates their interest. The conclusion should make an impression and support the idea or takeaway you wish to express. It might be a strong quotation, a thought-provoking question, or a call to action that inspires your audience to think or act.

Practice narrative elements including timing, tone, and delivery. To create a dynamic narrative, vary the speed of your story, choosing slower times for introspection and anticipation and quicker ones for thrill. To fit the atmosphere and emotions of your tale, adjust your tone. Take care with your delivery, whether it's written text, video, or audio, to ensure it adds to the narrative experience.

Finally, examine your audience's comments and involvement. Monitor the reaction to your tales and solicit feedback to see what connects with your target audience. Based on this input, adapt and enhance your storytelling strategies to consistently increase your capacity to engage and connect with your audience.

Leveraging Visuals and Aesthetics

Influencers may use images and aesthetics to improve their content, build a consistent brand identity, and engage their audience. Visual features may help draw the attention of consumers browsing through social media feeds and make your material more interesting and memorable. Influencers may successfully employ images and aesthetics to boost their online presence if they grasp their relevance.

Images, movies, graphics, and any other visual components that complement your information are examples of visuals. They assist in conveying your message, eliciting emotions, and leaving a lasting impact on your audience. Consider the graphics' relevancy to your material as well as their capacity to improve the overall story or theme. Choose images that are consistent with your brand and speak to the preferences and interests of your target audience.

The entire visual style and presentation of your material is referred to as aesthetics. Colors, typefaces, layouts, and design components are used to create a consistent and aesthetically appealing experience for your audience. Creating a consistent style helps to develop a recognizable brand identity and distinguishes you from others in your field.

Begin by developing your brand's visual identity. Consider the atmosphere, tone, and personality you want your graphics to communicate. Consider your target audience's preferences and match your aesthetics to their inclinations. For example, if your target audience values minimalism, choose clean and simple designs. Use strong and colorful colors to complement the tone of your content if it is about vibrant and dynamic issues.

When it comes to images and aesthetics, consistency is everything. Create a visual theme that runs across your material, including color palettes, typefaces, and general design aspects. Consistency produces a consistent and identifiable brand image, allowing your audience to recognize your material immediately.

Consider the quality of your graphics. Use clean and aesthetically attractive high-resolution photos and videos. Invest in high-quality photographic equipment or editing software, if applicable, to assure the quality of your graphics. Poor-quality images can detract from the meaning of your material and reduce its overall effect.

To interest your audience, try out several visual forms and narrative strategies. Include eye-catching photos or videos that pique visitors' interest and urge them to explore your information further. Use visuals or infographics to deliver complicated information in a visually appealing and readily accessible manner. In order to create a more immersive experience, incorporate storytelling techniques such as visual narratives or sequence of photographs.

Consider the platform-specific needs and aesthetic best practices. Each social networking site has its own set of graphic conventions and layouts. Understand the optimal dimensions, aspect ratios, and file formats for various platforms to guarantee that your images seem optimized and aesthetically attractive to your audience.

Keep up with current design trends and aesthetics. Investigate prominent visual styles, color palettes, and design aspects that are popular with your target demographic. Adapt and incorporate these trends into your content while keeping your distinct brand identity in mind.

Analyze the performance and engagement of your visual material on a regular basis. Monitor the stats and comments from your audience to determine which graphics have the most resonance and cause the most interaction. Adapt your visual strategy in response to these findings in order to continuously develop and polish your content.

Influencers may utilize visuals and aesthetics to boost their content and establish a unified and aesthetically attractive brand identity by leveraging visuals and aesthetics. Visuals are crucial in attracting attention and engaging your audience on social media, as users are continuously browsing through an overwhelming volume of material.

Visuals include a wide range of materials that complement your content, such as photographs, videos, graphics, and design elements. They are an important tool for communicating your message, eliciting emotions, and leaving a lasting impact on your audience. When choosing images, keep in mind their relevance to your material as well as their capacity to enrich the overall story or theme. Choose images that are consistent with your brand and speak to the preferences and interests of your target audience.

Aesthetics, on the other hand, refers to your content's overall visual style and presentation. It entails the deliberate selection and use of colors, typefaces, layouts, and design components that result in a unified and aesthetically appealing experience for your audience. Creating a consistent style not only helps to develop a recognizable business identity, but it also differentiates you from others in your field.

To effectively exploit visuals and aesthetics, begin by defining your brand's visual identity. Consider the atmosphere, tone, and personality you want your graphics to communicate. Consider your target audience's preferences and match your aesthetics to their inclinations. For example, if your target audience values minimalism, choose clean and simple designs. Use strong and colorful colors to complement the tone of your content if it is about vibrant and dynamic issues.

When it comes to using graphics and aesthetics, consistency is essential. Create a visual theme that runs across your material, including color palettes, typefaces, and general design aspects. Consistency produces a consistent and identifiable brand image, allowing your audience to recognize your material immediately. It promotes trust and familiarity while also reinforcing your brand's identity.

Another key factor to consider is quality. Use clean and aesthetically attractive high-resolution photos and videos. Invest in high-quality photographic equipment or editing software, if applicable, to assure the quality of your graphics. Poor-quality images can detract from the meaning of your material and reduce its overall effect.

To interest your audience, try out several visual forms and narrative strategies. Include eye-catching photos or videos that pique visitors' interest and urge them to explore your information further. Use visuals or infographics to deliver complicated information in a visually appealing and readily accessible manner. Investigate the power of visual storytelling by creating an immersive experience for your audience by utilizing a sequence of photographs or films that form a cohesive tale.

It is critical to consider platform-specific needs and visual best practices. Each social networking site has its own set of graphic conventions and layouts. Understanding the optimal dimensions, aspect ratios, and file formats for various platforms can guarantee that your images seem optimized and aesthetically attractive to your audience.

Keep up with current design trends and aesthetics. Investigate prominent visual styles, color palettes, and design aspects that are popular with your target demographic. While being loyal to your distinct brand identity is crucial, adopting parts of current trends may help keep your images fresh and interesting.

Analyze the performance and engagement of your visual material on a regular basis. Track analytics like likes, comments, shares, and click-through rates, and solicit feedback from your audience. This data will reveal which graphics resonate the most with your audience and generate the greatest interaction. Adapt your visual strategy in response to these findings in order to continuously develop and polish your content.

Influencers may elevate their content, build a strong brand identity, and attract the attention of their audience in the congested social media landscape by skillfully using images and aesthetics. Visual aspects enhance the visual appeal, memory, and shareability of your material, allowing you to stand out and leave a lasting impression. You may develop a unified brand image and a devoted following of engaged and visually captivated followers by using a consistent and aesthetically engaging look.

Chapter 5: Building an Engaged Community

Understanding Your Target Audience

Understanding your target audience is essential for becoming a successful influencer. Your target audience is the group of individuals you want to reach, engage, and influence with your content. Gaining a thorough understanding of your target audience allows you to adjust your content, message, and techniques in order to effectively engage with them and establish a devoted following.

Begin by completing extensive research on your target audience. Determine the demographic factors that identify your audience, such as age, gender, geography, and employment. Investigate their interests, preferences, and behaviors to learn more about what appeals to them. Use analytics tools, surveys, or social media insights to collect data and assess your existing audience's demographics and interaction habits.

Create buyer personas or audience profiles for your desired audience groups. Beyond demographic information, these personas should go into psychographic factors such as their values, motivations, difficulties, and ambitions. Creating comprehensive personas allows you to personalize your audience and gain a deeper understanding of their wants and desires.

Directly communicate with your audience via social media interactions, comments, and direct messaging. Pay close attention to their comments, questions, and concerns. Take note of the conversations taking place around your content and within your specialty. This personal connection provides you with unique insights and viewpoints, as well as the opportunity to create relationships with your audience.

Use data and analytics to have a better knowledge of your target audience. Track engagement indicators like as likes, comments, shares, and click-through rates with social media analytics. Analyze which forms of content work best and have the most impact on your audience. Examine the data for patterns and trends to determine what appeals to your target audience and change your content strategy accordingly.

Keep current with industry trends and changes in your field. Investigate what subjects, issues, or trends are currently relevant and interesting to your target audience. This enables you to provide timely and valuable content that meets their demands and puts you at the front of their minds as a reliable source of information or inspiration.

To get direct input from your audience, use surveys or polls. Inquire about their preferences, thoughts, and what they want to see more of from you. This feedback gives you vital insights into their wishes and expectations, allowing you to improve your content and strategy to better meet their demands.

Keep an eye on and assess your rivals who are targeting a comparable audience. Examine their content, levels of interaction, and methods. Identify gaps or possibilities for differentiation and providing unique value to your target audience. Understanding your rivals' strategies may also assist you in staying updated about industry developments and staying ahead of the curve.

Revisit and improve your understanding of your target audience on a regular basis. Your audience's requirements and tastes may vary as they grow and expand. Seek feedback on a regular basis, analyze engagement numbers, and adjust your strategy as needed to ensure your content remains current and connects with your audience.

You may develop content that speaks directly to your target audience's interests, issues, and objectives by understanding them. This strengthens your relationship, creates trust, and positions you as a valued resource or expert in your field. Finally, identifying your target audience helps you to adjust your content and techniques to engage and influence them successfully, resulting in long-term success as an influencer.

Strategies for Increasing Engagement

Increased engagement strategies are critical for influencers aiming to establish a loyal and engaged following. The interactions, emotions, and participation of your audience with your material are referred to as engagement. You can develop a feeling of community, inspire meaningful connections, and create a good and engaging online environment by using successful tactics. Here are some ideas for enhancing participation:

Produce valuable and high-quality material: Make an effort to offer information that is instructive, entertaining, or inspirational. Share insights, advice, or funny anecdotes that are relevant to your audience's interests and requirements. High-quality information is more likely to catch attention, inspire debate, and promote participation.

Understand your target audience: Understanding your target audience is essential for developing material that will appeal to them. Create material that is tailored to their tastes, interests, and communication style. When planning and creating content, keep their demographics, psychographics, and habits in mind.

urge interaction: Actively urge your audience to interact with and participate in your material. Pose questions, solicit feedback, or promote comments and debates. Encourage your audience to offer their experiences, anecdotes, or tips about your topic. Participate in discussions and reply to comments to develop a feeling of community.

Incorporate narrative tactics into your material to engage your readers and generate emotional relationships. Create relevant, honest, and intriguing storytelling. To keep your audience interested and willing to respond, use storytelling elements such as personal experiences, conflict, or resolve.

Collaborate with your audience: Allow your audience to contribute and be a part of the content development process. To include people in decision-making or content ideas, use polls, surveys, or contests. Display user-generated material and offer your audience credit for their contributions. Collaborating with your audience increases their sense of value and investment in your material.

Optimize for interactivity: To increase engagement, use interactive features and formats. To promote engagement, provide quizzes, polls, or interactive storytelling. Create chances for your audience to actively participate in your content rather than simply watching it.

Maintain consistency and frequency in your publishing schedule to keep your audience interested and informed. To keep their attention, present new information and updates on a regular basis. However, keep the quality of your material good, since consistency should not jeopardize the value you provide.

Use visual elements: Visuals are interesting and may draw attention. Include attention-grabbing photos, videos, or graphics in your article. Make your message more remembered and shared by using images to supplement and enhance it.

Cross-promote your material on numerous channels: Promote your content and drive engagement on many platforms. Share samples or teasers on one site while linking to the complete material on another. This cross-promotion broadens your audience and motivates followers from many platforms to interact with your material.

Be genuine and responsive: Display your true personality and connect on a personal level with your audience. Respond to comments, mails, and enquiries as soon as possible. Developing genuine relationships with your target audience promotes trust, loyalty, and continuing engagement.

Analyze and adapt: Analyze engagement data and feedback on a regular basis to learn what content works well and connects with your audience. Use these insights to improve your content strategy by detecting gaps and experimenting with different ways.

Understanding your audience, producing great content, and actively promoting involvement are all necessary for increasing engagement. Implementing these tactics will allow you to build a lively and engaged audience that actively interacts with your material, promoting your development and success as an influencer.

Utilizing Collaboration and Networking

Collaboration and networking are effective strategies for influencers aiming to broaden their reach, make significant relationships, and improve their content. Collaboration entails collaborating with other producers, companies, or individuals to develop collaborative content, cross-promote each other, or collaborate on projects together. Networking entails making contacts and developing relationships with other influencers, industry experts, and like-minded people. Influencers may reach new audiences, get visibility, and form mutually advantageous collaborations by skillfully harnessing cooperation and networking.

Collaboration has various advantages. It enables you to mix your experience, creativity, and audience reach with the expertise, creativity, and audience reach of others, resulting in unique and captivating content. Collaborating with like-minded influencers or complimentary companies might help you reach new audiences interested in your content. It allows for the sharing of knowledge, learning, and progress as you obtain insights from people in your industry.

To begin partnerships, look for possible partners that share your beliefs, specialization, or target audience. Look for creators or companies who can compliment your content and give value to your audience. Contact them with a well-crafted proposal emphasizing mutual benefits and prospective partnership prospects.

Collaborations may take many forms, including collaborative films, podcasts, blog posts, social media takeovers, and product partnerships. Choose the format that best matches your material and the collaboration's aims. Depending on the aims and desires of all parties involved, collaborative initiatives can range from one-time collaborations to long-term relationships.

Networking is essential for developing contacts and increasing your influencer network. Attend industry events, conferences, or meetings to network with other industry influencers, brand reps, and experts. Participate in conversations, exchange ideas, and make meaningful connections. Networking gives you access to a multitude of knowledge, insights, and possibilities in your field.

Social media platforms are very useful for networking. Like, comment on, and share the material of other influencers. Join relevant forums or organizations where you may engage with people who share your interests. Collaborate with people in your network by highlighting each other's content, taking part in shout-outs, or conducting collaborative live sessions. Social media networking allows you to broaden your visibility and interact with people who have similar interests and ambitions.

When cooperating or networking, it is critical to approach the situation with an open and mutually beneficial perspective. Seek chances for mutual advantage, such as reaching a new audience, getting publicity, or exchanging knowledge. Be willing to explore ideas, compromise, and find common ground. Building genuine connections based on trust and respect is critical for long-term and successful cooperation.

Assess and analyze the consequences of your partnerships and networking activities on a regular basis. Analyze engagement data, audience growth, and audience comments to determine the impact of partnerships. Consider the benefits of networking connections, such as fresh ideas, collaboration prospects, or personal development. Based on these observations and learnings, modify your strategy.

Influencers may reach new audiences, increase their reach, and get visibility through collaborating and networking. Influencers may generate captivating content, learn from others, and make significant relationships by collaborating with other artists, companies, or industry professionals. Influencers may stimulate development, build a strong presence, and open doors to new opportunities in the influencer arena by collaborating and networking.

Chapter 6: Optimizing Your Social Media Profiles

Crafting Captivating Bios and Profiles

Creating engaging biographies and profiles is a critical component of establishing a strong online presence as an influencer. Your bio and biography serve as an introduction to your brand and play an important part in catching your audience's interest. You may make a captivating and unforgettable impression by deliberately constructing your bio and biography, enticing readers to explore your material further.

Begin by learning about your intended audience. Determine your audience's demographics, interests, and preferences. Customize your language, tone, and messaging to meet their needs and interests. This allows you to write a bio and biography that speaks directly to your target audience's wants.

Introduce yourself succinctly and effectively. Begin with your name or the name by which you are most often known. You can also incorporate a memorable phrase or slogan that summarizes your speciality, skill, or unique selling point. This provides as a brief overview of what you have to offer and attracts customers' attention.

Emphasize your skills and distinct value offer. Communicate your area of expertise, highlight your talents, and underline what distinguishes you from others in your field. Use persuasion to properly convey the value you provide your audience. Concentrate on the advantages they will gain from following your material and how you can assist them.

To improve discoverability, use relevant keywords and hashtags. Consider the keywords and hashtags that your target audience is likely to use in their searches. This enhances the likelihood that your bio and profile will show in relevant search results, attracting individuals who are interested in your content.

Tell your narrative succinctly and engagingly. Use your bio to emphasize essential components of your influencer journey, such as milestones, successes, or experiences relevant to your expertise and audience. Establish a connection with your audience by displaying honesty and individuality.

Use emojis and formatting to make your bio more visually attractive and easier to read. Emojis may be used to inject personality and break up content, while formatting methods such as line breaks, bullet points, and space can assist organize information and highlight crucial points.

Include a clear call to action to entice people to act. This might include encouraging people to follow your account, visit your website, see certain material, or participate in a specific activity. The call to action should be consistent with your aims and direct people to further connect with your business.

Display social evidence, such as logos of respected firms with which you have cooperated or mentions of media appearances. This establishes credibility and trust with your audience, suggesting that you are a well-known and respected influencer in your sector.

As your brand matures and flourishes, check and update your bio and profile on a regular basis. To create a unified and identifiable identity, keep your messaging and branding consistent across all media.

Making compelling biographies and profiles involves careful consideration of your target audience, message, and branding. By giving these factors some attention, you can produce a fascinating and memorable introduction that draws and engages your audience, laying the groundwork for meaningful relationships and long-term success as an influencer.

Utilizing Keywords and Hashtags

Influencers must properly use keywords and hashtags to promote discoverability, attract a larger audience, and increase the exposure of their material. Keywords and hashtags serve as search keywords and classification aids, assisting users in discovering relevant material and allowing influencers to interact with their target audience. Influencers may optimize their content for search engines and social media platforms by integrating relevant keywords and hashtags, boosting their chances of being found by those interested in their field.

Keywords are words or phrases that reflect your content's core subjects, ideas, or notions. They are the phrases that consumers are likely to use while searching for certain information or material. Keyword research is essential for identifying the most relevant and popular terms in your field. Tools like as Google Keyword Planner, SEMrush, and Moz Keyword Explorer may help you uncover high-ranking keywords that are relevant to your content and target audience.

Include keywords naturally in your material, such as your bio, captions, titles, and descriptions. Incorporate keywords into your meta tags, headers, and body material to optimize your website or blog. This assists search engines in determining the relevancy of your material to user searches, hence increasing your exposure in search engine results.

In contrast, hashtags are particular terms or phrases prefixed by the "#" mark. They aid in the categorization and grouping of information on social media sites, making it simpler for users to find similar postings. Hashtags enable you to incorporate your material in relevant hashtag feeds, enhancing its visibility to people who follow or search for certain hashtags.

Investigate popular and relevant hashtags in your niche. Look for hashtags that are commonly used by your target audience or that correspond to the themes you cover. Consider incorporating trending hashtags related to current events or popular topics as well. To reach a certain audience, strike a balance between utilizing wide hashtags with high search traffic and more specific specialty hashtags.

Incorporate hashtags into your content wisely. Include them in your captions, comments, and even your post's aesthetic aspects. Overuse of hashtags, on the other hand, might make your material look spammy or eager for attention. To retain readability, limit the amount of hashtags you use and make sure they are related to the material you are sharing.

It's critical to employ keywords and hashtags consistently across platforms and content. Create a list of important keywords and hashtags that correspond to your brand and content emphasis. This consistency contributes to the development of your brand identity and makes it simpler for people to identify certain phrases or hashtags with your content.

Analytic tools may be used to track the performance and engagement of your content. Monitor the reach, impressions, and interaction of your posts including certain keywords or hashtags. This information can assist you in determining which keywords or hashtags are generating the greatest awareness and interaction, allowing you to fine-tune your approach over time.

Keep an eye out for hot topics and conversations in your niche. In order to join the conversation and enhance your exposure among those interested in these issues, including relevant keywords or hashtags connected to these trends. This helps you to keep current and capitalize on trendy topics.

Influencers may increase the exposure of their material, attract a larger audience, and interact with consumers interested in their field by successfully leveraging keywords and hashtags. Influencers may optimize their content for search engines and social media platforms by adding important keywords organically and utilizing smart hashtags. This increases the odds of getting noticed by their target audience.

Enhancing Discoverability and SEO

Improving discoverability and SEO (Search Engine Optimization) is critical for influencers seeking to boost their online presence and attract a larger audience. The capacity of consumers to locate your material via search engines, social media platforms, or other online channels is referred to as discoverability. SEO, on the other hand, is improving your content and online presence to rank higher on search engine results pages, increasing the likelihood that users will find your material. Influencers may draw more organic traffic and build their following by concentrating on improving discoverability and using efficient SEO methods.

Consider the following tactics to improve discoverability and SEO:

Conduct extensive keyword research to determine the terms and phrases that consumers in your niche are searching for. To locate high-ranking and relevant keywords, use keyword research tools such as Google Keyword Planner, SEMrush, or Moz Keyword Explorer. Include these keywords in your content naturally, including titles, headers, captions, and descriptions.

Optimize your website or blog: If you have a website or blog, make it search engine friendly. On-page SEO factors such as meta tags, meta descriptions, URLs, and headers should be taken into account. In these elements, include relevant keywords to assist search engines comprehend the content and increase your ranking in search results.

Produce high-quality content: Concentrate on creating relevant and interesting material that addresses the needs and interests of your target audience. Content that is useful, relevant, and well-structured is prioritized by search engines. Incorporate keywords naturally into your material, making sure they flow smoothly and don't interfere with reading or user experience.

Optimize for mobile: With the growing popularity of mobile devices, it's critical that your website and content be mobile-friendly. Optimize the style and layout of your website to deliver a consistent surfing experience across all devices. Mobile optimization is vital not just for user experience but also for search engine rankings, as mobile-friendly websites are prioritized by search engines.

Create high-quality backlinks: Backlinks, which are links to your content from other credible websites, are a significant aspect in SEO. Seek chances to develop high-quality backlinks by cooperating with other industry influencers or media, guest blogging on relevant websites, or attending industry events. Backlinks of high quality indicate to search engines that your material is reliable and useful.

Use internal linking: Internal linking is the practice of connecting relevant sites or articles within your own website or blog. This assists search engines in comprehending the structure of your website and enhances user experience by directing readers to relevant information. Internal links should be deliberately placed throughout your content, linking pertinent sites and articles.

Optimize your social media profiles: Social media platforms are very important for discoverability. Improve the visibility of your social media profiles by using important keywords in your bio, descriptions, and captions. Make smart use of hashtags to classify your content and boost its visibility on the site.

Analyze and refine on a regular basis: Use analytics tools to track your website traffic, engagement metrics, and search rankings. Analyze the performance of your content, see patterns, and learn about user behavior. Use this information to fine-tune your content strategy, find areas for improvement, and tweak your SEO strategies.

Keep up with SEO best practices: SEO algorithms and best practices are always changing. Keep up with the newest trends, algorithm tweaks, and SEO tactics. Stay involved in SEO networks, read industry blogs, and follow trustworthy SEO gurus to guarantee your techniques are up to date.

To improve discoverability and SEO, a mix of keyword research, content optimization, technological concerns, and continual analysis is required. Influencers may increase their online exposure, generate organic traffic, and reach a larger audience by applying successful techniques and staying up to current on SEO developments. Remember that SEO is a long-term endeavor, and regular optimization and refining are critical to obtaining long-term success.

Chapter 7: Partnering with Brands and Collaborations

Approaching Brand Collaborations

Approaching brand collaborations is a critical step for influencers aiming to form mutually beneficial partnerships and broaden their reach. Working with corporations or brands to provide sponsored content, promote products or services, or cooperate on marketing initiatives is what brand cooperation entails. These collaborations may give influencers with income options, greater audience exposure, and the potential to identify themselves with recognized businesses. When considering brand collaborations, keep the following procedures in mind:

Define your brand and audience: Before approaching businesses, have a clear grasp of your own brand identity, values, and audience interests. This assists you in identifying companies that are relevant to your specialty and resonate with your target audience. With a solid brand identity, you may approach partnerships that are real and truly valuable to your fans.

Investigate and pick appropriate brands: Conduct extensive research to find companies that match your beliefs, specialty, and target audience. Consider brand repute, product relevancy, and the audience that you both serve. Look for businesses who are genuinely interested in working with influencers and have a track record of successful collaborations.

Familiarize yourself with the brand: Before reaching out, become acquainted with its products, services, and messaging. Learn about their brand philosophy, target demographic, and prior collaborations. With this information, you will be able to adapt your approach and demonstrate your comprehension and interest in their business.

Create a great proposal: When approaching businesses, create a customized and captivating pitch that emphasizes the unique value you provide to the cooperation. Explain how your audience fits the brand's target demographic and how your content may successfully market their products or services. To illustrate your experience and potential effect, showcase your inventiveness, engagement data, and prior successful partnerships.

Ideas for collaboration: Provide concrete partnership ideas that demonstrate your innovation while also aligning with the brand's aims. Customize your ideas to capitalize on your talents and the distinct value you offer to the cooperation. Consider the brand's goals, such as new releases, seasonal campaigns, or specialized marketing activities, and suggest ways you might help them succeed.

Display your professionalism by: Maintain a professional demeanor throughout the collaborative process. Respond to contact immediately, display dependability, and keep clear and open channels of communication. Influencers that are organized, detail-oriented, and able to fulfill deadlines are valued by brands. Demonstrate your dedication to creating high-quality content and exceeding the brand's expectations.

Negotiate terms and expectations: Once a brand expresses interest in working, negotiate the partnership's conditions and expectations. Compensation, deliverables, deadlines, usage rights, and any contractual agreements are all included. Make your expectations explicit and ensure that both sides grasp the terms of the partnership.

Create authentic and engaging content: When carrying out the cooperation, prioritize the creation of content that is authentic, aligned with your brand, and connects with your target audience. Make it clear that the collaboration is sponsored material, and make certain that your messaging stays authentic and loyal to your beliefs. Prioritize providing value to your audience while reaching the goals of the brand.

Evaluate and cultivate relationships: Following the partnership, assess its success and influence. Analyze engagement analytics, audience input, and brand satisfaction. Maintain a professional and positive connection with the brand, even if the cooperation is just temporary. Relationship building can lead to future partnerships or recommendations to other companies.

Brand collaborations need research, planning, and excellent communication. By associating yourself with appropriate businesses and providing high-quality content, you can build long-term connections and collaborations that benefit both you and the brand. Throughout the collaborative process, remember to retain professionalism, sincerity, and a focus on providing value to your audience.

Negotiating Contracts and Compensation

When it comes to brand collaborations, influencers must negotiate contracts and incentives. It entails negotiating with the brand to set mutually acceptable conditions and financial remuneration for the collaboration. The negotiating step is critical because it ensures that all parties are pleased with the agreement and understand their respective roles and responsibilities.

Influencers should approach the negotiating process with professionalism, clarity, and a solid awareness of their worth in the relationship. Here's an explanation of how to use a continuous text to negotiate contracts and compensation:

Before getting into contract discussions, influencers gather all relevant information about the company and its goals. This involves investigating the brand's target demographic, products or services, and any unique marketing objectives. This data assists influencers in aligning their suggestions and comprehending how their material might benefit the company.

Following that, influencers specify their deliverables and describe exactly what they will contribute as part of the engagement. This includes defining the sort of material they will produce, the quantity or frequency with which they will post, and any other services they will provide, such as attending events or engaging in promotional efforts. Influencers and companies may guarantee they are on the same page and minimize miscommunications by explicitly identifying deliverables.

Influencers debate remuneration throughout the negotiating process. They give their recommended cost structure based on their influencer worth, taking into account the size of their following, engagement rates, content quality, and past partnerships. The suggested pay should be proportionate to the work, time, and resources necessary to develop the content, as well as the potential influence on the brand's target audience. Influencers may also consider aspects like as exclusivity and usage rights for the material when determining pay.

Negotiation entails an open and courteous communication between the brand representative and the influencer. Both sides should feel free to communicate their hopes and worries. The negotiating process may include back-and-forth conversations, making concessions, and reaching an agreement that is acceptable to both parties. It is critical to resolve any misunderstandings or questions, obtain clarity on contractual provisions, and ensure that everyone is on the same page about the collaboration's expectations.

A formal contract is normally prepared once both parties have agreed on the conditions and pay. The contract specifies the agreed-upon conditions, deliverables, pay, timetable, and any other elements that may be applicable. Influencers may choose to have legal counsel analyze the contract to ensure that their rights and interests are safeguarded.

Contract and remuneration negotiations necessitate efficient communication, professionalism, and a clear understanding of the influencer's worth. Influencers may develop effective brand relationships that connect with their aims and give fair pay for their work by participating in serious talks and negotiating a mutually beneficial arrangement.

Maintaining Authenticity in Brand Partnerships

Maintaining authenticity in brand collaborations is critical for influencers to develop trust with their audience and maintain the integrity of their own brand. The attribute of being real, truthful, and true to oneself is referred to as authenticity. When influencers work with businesses, it's critical that the collaboration connects with their ideals, resonates with their audience, and does not jeopardize their authenticity. Using a continuous text, here is an explanation of the notion of retaining authenticity in brand partnerships:

The foundation of a successful influencer's profession is authenticity. It forges a deep bond with the audience, establishing trust and credibility. Influencers should carefully assess whether the cooperation resonates with their own brand and beliefs before getting into brand relationships. Staying loyal to oneself and having a constant voice, style, and material that connects with the audience are required for authenticity.

Influencers should undertake extensive research on the brand and its products or services before entering into brand collaborations. They should ensure that the brand's values are compatible with their own and that the cooperation provides actual value to their target audience. It's vital to remember that audience trust is earned over time, and collaborating with businesses that don't share the influencer's beliefs might undermine that trust.

Influencers should properly convey their expectations and boundaries to the company throughout the negotiating process. This includes talking about content restrictions, messaging, and any other needs that will help them preserve their authenticity. Communication that is open and honest is essential for developing a partnership that respects the influencer's creative freedom while meeting the brand's goals.

Influencers should aim to keep their own voice and style when generating sponsored material. Their own experiences, views, and genuine excitement for the brand's products or services should be reflected in the material. Personal anecdotes, stories, or observations can assist keep the influencer's authenticity while also making the material more relevant to their audience.

Maintaining authenticity requires transparency. When material is sponsored or a connection exists, influencers should make it obvious. Authentic influencers recognize the value of being open and honest with their audience because it fosters trust and credibility. Influencers should adhere to legal and ethical disclosure rules to ensure that their audience is informed of any potential biases.

Influencers should emphasize their audience's demands and interests even while working with brands. They should think about how the partnership will help their audience and deliver useful material that meets their audience's expectations. Influencers must be aware of their audience's input and adapt their approach accordingly in order to keep the trust they have earned.

Authenticity in brand collaborations necessitates ongoing assessment and review. Influencers should evaluate their collaborations on a regular basis to ensure that they are consistent with their brand values and continue to resonate with their audience. If a brand partnership jeopardizes authenticity, influencers must have the confidence to refuse or rethink the agreement in order to keep their integrity.

Influencers may deepen their relationship with their audience, develop their personal brand, and achieve long-term success by being honest in brand engagements. Influencers gain a dedicated following and become trusted influencers in their particular niches when they remain true to themselves, produce real material, and prioritize the interests of their audience.

Maintaining authenticity in brand collaborations entails more than simply aligning ideals and producing real content. Here are some more factors to consider while attempting to retain authenticity:

Choosing the correct brand partners: Select companies that are compatible with your specialty, values, and target demographic. Look for businesses that actually match your content and resonate with the interests of your target audience. It becomes simpler to develop real content that effortlessly connects with your existing content strategy by working with businesses that are a natural match.

Long-term partnerships: Establishing long-term ties with brands enables for more collaboration and comprehension. Long-term relationships build trust and provide influencers more creative flexibility while connecting their ideals with the brand's goals. Brands that embrace authenticity and engage in long-term relationships are more likely to support and respect the creative vision of an influencer.

Communication transparency: Maintain open and transparent communication with brand partners. To keep brand collaborations authentic and current, clearly convey your audience's choices, interests, and comments. Create a solid communication channel in which both sides may freely communicate their problems, opinions, and ideas. This contributes to the creation of a collaborative atmosphere that values honesty.

Tell tales that are real to your experiences and that resonate with your audience. Include personal experiences, reveal behind-the-scenes information, and emphasize the real-world effect of the brand's products or services. Authentic storytelling fosters a stronger connection with your audience and lends credibility to your brand collaboration.

Balance promotional and non-promotional content: While brand collaborations entail the advertising of products or services, it is critical to maintain a balance of non-promotional material. To establish a true relationship with your audience, blend organic and paid content. This prevents brand collaborations from overpowering your own voice and content.

Maintain your values: Always put your ideals and principles first. Avoid relationships that contradict or jeopardize your essential convictions. Because your audience connects with your authenticity, it's critical that you preserve your integrity by only cooperating with businesses that share similar beliefs.

Engage your audience: Actively engage your audience and solicit feedback on brand relationships. Listen to their issues, address them, and include them in decision-making processes. You may better understand your audience's expectations and ensure that brand collaborations correspond with their interests by including them.

Regularly analyze partnerships: analyze the efficacy and impact of your brand relationships on a regular basis. Examine the comments, engagement analytics, and audience sentiment surrounding your collaborations on a regular basis. Check to see whether the partnerships are still connecting with your audience and reaching your goals. Consider changing or terminating a cooperation if it no longer seems honest or provides value.

Keeping brand connections real demands continual work and dedication. It's a fine line between satisfying the brand's goals and remaining genuine to yourself and your audience. You can build brand collaborations that authentically represent your beliefs and engage with your audience by selecting the proper brand partners, speaking clearly, adopting authentic storytelling, and remaining connected with your audience.

Chapter 8: Leveraging Affiliate Marketing and Sponsorships

Exploring Affiliate Marketing Programs

Investigating affiliate marketing networks allows influencers to monetize their content and earn commissions by endorsing companies or services. Affiliate marketing is a performance-based marketing technique in which affiliates receive a reward for driving sales or generating leads for a business via their unique affiliate links. This notion enables influencers to monetize their following and influence by endorsing products or services they sincerely believe in.

Influencers should take the following actions to properly investigate affiliate marketing programs:

Investigate and choose affiliate programs: Begin by looking into reliable affiliate programs that are relevant to your topic, audience, and personal brand. Look for programs offered by businesses you know and whose products or services are relevant to your target demographic. Consider commission rates, cookie length (the amount of time affiliates can earn a commission), and program support.

Join affiliate networks: Affiliate networks are platforms that link influencers with a variety of affiliate programs in a variety of sectors. Joining these networks gives you access to a wide pool of businesses and makes it easier to identify acceptable affiliate programs. Amazon Associates, ShareASale, and CJ Affiliate are some major affiliate networks.

Examine the terms and conditions: Before enrolling in an affiliate program, thoroughly read the terms and conditions. Learn about the program's qualifications, limitations, and promotional rules. Take note of any exclusivity conditions, restrictions on promotion channels, or special rules governing disclosure and compliance with applicable requirements.

Choose appropriate items or services: Choose affiliate items or services that are relevant to your audience's interests and requirements. Promoting items that are relevant to your expertise and resonate with your target audience increases the credibility of your recommendations. To keep your audience's confidence, prioritize quality and value.

Create interesting content: Create intriguing content that revolves on the items or services you're marketing. Create insightful reviews, tutorials, comparisons, or suggestions that emphasize the goods' benefits and characteristics. In order to add authenticity and credibility to your advice, use personal experiences or tales. Visual material like photos or movies may also boost engagement.

Transparency is key in affiliate marketing, therefore disclose affiliate ties. Make your affiliate affiliations clear to your readers in a prominent and intelligible manner. This may be accomplished by including disclaimers in blog posts, captions, or separate disclosure pages on your website. Maintaining trust with your audience requires adhering to ethical norms and revealing your ties.

Strategically distribute affiliate links: Integrate your affiliate links naturally into your article. Make sure the links are clickable and trackable. To reach diverse sectors of your audience and optimize your earning potential, use a range of promotional channels such as blog articles, social networking platforms, newsletters, or YouTube videos.

Track and evaluate performance: Use monitoring tools offered by the affiliate program or affiliate network to monitor your affiliate marketing performance. Keep track of your clicks, conversions, and commission revenue. Analyze the data to see which goods or types of content create the most engagement and conversions, allowing you to fine-tune your strategy and maximize your affiliate marketing efforts.

Maintaining excellent relationships with the products you represent as an affiliate is essential. Communicate with the affiliate program management or support teams of the company, provide feedback, and look for options for collaboration or unique offers for your audience. Building great relationships can result in extra perks such as higher commission rates, unique promotions, or first access to new products.

refine your affiliate marketing efforts: To maximize your earning potential, you should always refine your affiliate marketing techniques. Experiment with various advertising strategies, content formats, and platforms to determine which ones perform best for your target demographic. Track the performance of several campaigns, experiment with different messaging or images, and adjust your strategy based on the results. To enhance engagement and conversions, always improve your content and advertising efforts.

vary affiliate relationships: To vary your affiliate partnerships, look into cooperation with a variety of businesses and goods. This reduces your reliance on a single brand or program, reduces risks, and enables you to appeal to diverse sectors of your audience. Diversification also gives you with a broader selection of items and services to promote, allowing you to respond to your audience's different interests and requirements.

Keep up with industry trends: Affiliate marketing is an ever-changing sector, with new trends, technology, and laws appearing all the time. Keep up to date on industry advancements, affiliate marketing best practices, and any regulatory changes that may influence your promotional activity. By remaining current, you can adjust your methods and capitalize on new possibilities as they occur.

Maintain transparency and trust: In affiliate marketing, transparency is essential. Remind your readers of your affiliate partnerships on a regular basis, and mention your membership in affiliate programs. Sincerity fosters trust among your audience members, ensuring that they understand your objectives and identify your advice as genuine. Avoid information that is false or unduly promotional, since this may jeopardize your credibility.

Participate with your audience: Engage your audience actively to learn about their requirements, preferences, and feedback on the items or services you advertise. Respond to comments, messages, and enquiries as soon as possible, indicating your dedication to delivering value and supporting the interests of your audience. You may better adjust your affiliate marketing efforts to fulfill their expectations if you maintain a solid connection.

Monitor and review affiliate programs: Review the performance of the affiliate programs in which you are participating on a regular basis. Examine if the programs continue to fit with the interests of your target audience, as well as their commission rates, payment dependability, and quality of support. If a program no longer satisfies your requirements or becomes less successful over time, look into other programs that provide greater prospects.

Maintain regulatory compliance: Follow the rules and regulations that govern affiliate marketing in your jurisdiction. To guarantee that your promotional efforts are lawful, familiarize yourself with regulations governing advertising, disclosures, and consumer protection. This includes knowing your region's disclosure duties, content labeling, and any limits on advertising techniques.

Seek expert help if necessary: If you have questions concerning the legal or financial elements of affiliate marketing, you should speak with a professional, such as a lawyer, an accountant, or an experienced affiliate marketer. They can advise you on contractual agreements, tax duties, financial management, and any legal consequences that may arise as a result of your affiliate marketing operations. Professional assistance can assist you in navigating complicated challenges while remaining within legal and ethical constraints.

Influencers may develop a consistent revenue stream while providing helpful suggestions to their audience by studying affiliate marketing networks intelligently, maximizing your efforts, and preserving openness and trust. Building long-term success in influencer marketing, like any other component, necessitates a focus on authenticity, audience engagement, and ongoing adaptability to industry changes and laws.

Maximizing Sponsorship Opportunities

Maximizing sponsorship possibilities is a critical step in an influencer's path to effectively monetize their platform and create solid connections with businesses. It entails exploiting your influence, content, and audience to establish and maximize sponsorship deals. Influencers may get a variety of benefits by utilizing sponsorship possibilities, including cash reward, exposure to new audiences, and access to unique items or events.

Influencers should take a deliberate and aggressive approach to maximize sponsorship possibilities. Here's how it's done:

First and foremost, you must understand your own brand and target demographic. Define your influencer niche, values, and the unique value you bring to the table. This self-awareness will assist you in identifying the brands and relationships that are compatible with your identity and connect with your target audience. You boost your chances of getting sponsors that respect your authenticity by being true to your brand.

Following that, perform extensive study to locate possible sponsors. Investigate brands that share your target demographic and are related to your niche or content subject. Analyze their marketing strategy, current campaigns, and previous cooperation to learn about their beliefs and goals. This research will allow you to contact sponsors with a customized pitch that showcases your knowledge of their brand and target demographic.

When approaching sponsors, focus on developing genuine relationships. Create tailored and appealing proposals that emphasize your distinct value to their business. Explain how your target audience will benefit from the cooperation and demonstrate your inventiveness in incorporating their products or services into your content. Strive to provide a win-win scenario, stressing the mutual benefit and progress that can be realized via collaboration.

Develop compelling and authentic sponsored content in collaboration with sponsors. Maintain your own voice and style while tailoring your approach to suit with the brand's goals and messaging. Be open and honest with your audience about sponsored content to ensure that your suggestions and endorsements are authentic and trustworthy. To maximize the effect of sponsored content, you must balance the brand's aims with your authenticity.

Investigate potential for long-term collaborations with sponsors. Building long-term connections enables for deeper brand integration into your content, builds trust and credibility, and provides access to exclusive collaborations and higher pay. You increase your chances of future sponsorship opportunities by constantly offering value and meeting or surpassing the brand's expectations.

Diversify your strategy to enhance sponsorship chances. Consider product placements, ambassador programs, sponsored events or vacations, and sponsored social media campaigns. Diversification enables you to cater to many companies, target various parts of your audience, and demonstrate your adaptability as an influencer.

Evaluate the success of your sponsorships on a regular basis. Keep track of crucial data like as engagement rates, click-through rates, conversion rates, and audience feedback. Examine how sponsorships affect your growth, brand affiliation, and audience sentiment. With this data-driven strategy, you can fine-tune your plans, maximize future sponsorships, and demonstrate your value to new sponsors.

Finally, never undervalue the value of networking and industry relationships. Attend industry events, network with other influencers, and form partnerships with marketing and public relations experts. Collaboration with other influencers or collaborating with agencies can introduce you to new sponsorship options while also providing useful insights and assistance.

Influencers may optimize sponsorship possibilities and form beneficial collaborations with businesses by taking a smart and aggressive approach. Influencers may get lucrative sponsorships that not only produce cash but also help to their growth and success as influential content creators through authentic content production, personalized pitches, long-term relationship building, and continuing assessment.

Disclosure and Ethical Considerations

When it comes to brand collaborations and sponsored content, influencers must emphasize transparency and ethical concerns. These issues concentrate around maintaining openness, adhering to legal and industry norms, and protecting the influencer-audience relationship's trust and legitimacy.

whether it comes to disclosure, influencers must make it apparent to their audience whether their material is sponsored or involves a collaboration with a company. Transparency is essential in developing an open and honest relationship with your audience. Disclosures can take many different forms, including clear disclosures within captions, hashtags such as #ad or #sponsored, and dedicated disclosure pages on websites or platforms. The disclosure should be visible, understandable, and easily available to the audience.

Beyond disclosure, ethical issues include the influencer's entire conduct and ideals. Influencers must be cautious about the material they develop and promote, ensuring that it is consistent with their own ideas, values, and the interests of their target audience. Their decision-making should be guided by authenticity and honesty. It is critical to carefully examine brand collaborations, choosing ones that truly resonate with the influencer and add value to their audience. Collaborations should not jeopardize an influencer's reputation or dilute their own voice and style.

Furthermore, influencers must follow all applicable laws, advertising rules, and industry standards. Guidelines issued by regulatory authorities such as the Federal Trade Commission (FTC) in the United States or the Advertising Standards Authority (ASA) in the United Kingdom may be included. Influencers should be conversant with the disclosure standards, content labeling, and any regional rules or regulations governing sponsored material. Compliance with these rules ensures that influencers conduct themselves responsibly and transparently with their audience.

Influencers should examine the impact of their material on their audience in addition to transparency and legal compliance. They must be aware of their potential influence over their followers and utilize it appropriately. This includes refraining from deceptive activities, making false promises, and advocating dangerous items or habits. Influencers must emphasize their audience's well-being and best interests by delivering accurate information and engaging in good, meaningful dialogues.

Influencers may actively interact with their audience and promote open debate to reinforce ethical principles. They can solicit comments, listen to concerns, and answer to enquiries in a transparent manner. Influencers build trust and credibility with their audience by displaying a dedication to ethical standards and real connection.

For influencers to respect transparency and ethical considerations, regular self-reflection and review are required. They should evaluate their relationships, content strategy, and audience input on a regular basis to ensure that they are in line with their values and the expectations of their audience. Influencers should also remain up to date on developing ethical and legal trends, industry best practices, and regulatory developments in order to adjust their methods accordingly.

Influencers maintain openness, retain trust with their audience, and maintain their integrity as content providers by emphasizing disclosure and ethical issues. These elements are critical in developing a durable and acknowledged influencer presence and contribute to influencers' long-term success in the dynamic and ever-changing environment of digital media.

Chapter 9: Creating Your Own Products and Services

Identifying Profitable Product/Service Ideas

Finding lucrative product/service ideas is an important first step for entrepreneurs and aspiring company owners. It entails investigating market trends, customer demands, and prospective market gaps in order to identify opportunities with the potential for success and profitability.

Thorough market research is essential for identifying lucrative product/service concepts. Begin by researching current trends and patterns in your target market. Keep up to date on new sectors, technology breakthroughs, and altering customer tastes. You can find places where there is a need for new or enhanced products/services by identifying market gaps or neglected niches.

Understanding your target audience is also essential. Segment the market to find unique client demographics, wants, and pain areas. You may build ideas that cater to their individual requirements and create solutions that bring value to their lives by acquiring insights into their preferences, desires, and issues.

Brainstorming and idea generating are important steps in discovering profitable concepts. Encourage innovation and thinking beyond the box. Consider your own abilities, knowledge, and passions to generate ideas that are complementary to your talents and interests. Look for novel ways or unique combinations of current products/services that might provide you a market advantage.

Before committing time and money, it is critical to validate your ideas. To get input from potential consumers, conduct market surveys, interviews, or focus groups. This ensures that your product/service concept is appealing to the target audience and has a market.

It is also critical to research your competition. Analyze existing market products/services and assess their strengths, shortcomings, and pricing strategies. Determine strategies to distinguish yourself by providing unique value propositions or filling holes that rivals may have neglected.

Consider your ideas' viability and scalability. Examine the resources, infrastructure, and skills needed to bring your product or service to market. Examine your company idea's cost structure, prospective profit margins, and scalability.

Conduct an in-depth examination of market demand, competition, and financial predictions. This involves calculating market size, assessing future growth, and forecasting income and costs. Create a detailed business plan outlining your marketing approach, distribution networks, pricing, and customer acquisition strategies.

To identify successful product/service concepts, a mix of creativity, market research, understanding client demands, and meticulous analysis is required. You may improve your chances of generating effective and lucrative products/services by aligning your abilities, interests, and target market, as well as confirming your ideas. To increase your chances of success, remain open to feedback, be willing to iterate, and adjust your plans based on market conditions.

Developing and Launching Your Offering

Creating and releasing your offering is a vital step in making your product/service concept a reality. It entails developing your concept into a fully formed solution that fits the demands of customers and adds value to the market. By using a methodical strategy, you can assure a successful launch and lay the groundwork for long-term development and profitability.

The first stage in creating your service is to turn your concept into a precise strategy. Outline your product's or service's major features, functions, and advantages. Consider how it solves consumer issues or fulfills their aspirations. Create a clear value proposition that distinguishes your service from rivals and emphasizes its distinct selling qualities.

To test and validate your concept, construct a prototype or minimal viable product (MVP). This enables you to collect input from future clients and make required changes. Iterative design and development cycles should be used to continually enhance your product based on user input and market data.

Pay attention to criteria such as quality, usefulness, and dependability as you enhance your service. Strive to provide a consistent and satisfactory client experience. Investing in product design, user interface, packaging, or service delivery methods is one example. Align your product with industry standards and laws to secure compliance and consumer confidence.

Conduct market research to learn about the tastes, purchase habits, and price sensitivity of your target audience. This will assist you in determining the best price approach for your business. Consider production costs, price competition, and perceived value. Your pricing strategy should be in line with your target market and positioning.

Create an all-encompassing marketing and sales plan to raise awareness and attract consumers. To reach your target audience, use a variety of marketing channels such as digital marketing, social media, content production, and public relations. Create captivating messaging that explains the benefits and value of your service effectively. Use influencers, partnerships, or collaborations to increase your reach and reputation.

Make a go-to-market strategy including the major milestones, dates, and resources needed for a successful launch. This comprises logistics for manufacturing or service delivery, inventory management, distribution networks, and customer service. Consider scalability and expansion possibilities as you build systems and procedures to meet rising demand.

Prior to launch, extensively test your solution to verify it satisfies quality requirements and operates as planned. To fix any lingering concerns, get input from beta testers or early adopters. Prepare a strong customer support system to address enquiries, feedback, and possible difficulties that may develop following the launch.

Finally, use a well-thought-out launch strategy to generate attention and enthusiasm about your service. To stimulate anticipation and encourage early adoption, use pre-launch marketing, teasers, exclusive previews, or limited-time incentives. Engage your target audience at several touchpoints to make a good first impression and drive word-of-mouth recommendations.

Monitor the performance of your item once it has been launched on a regular basis. Collect client feedback, track sales, and assess key performance indicators to determine success and areas for development. Respond to market conditions and changing client wants by modifying your product and marketing techniques.

Creating and releasing your service necessitates a methodical approach, a focus on quality, and a thorough grasp of your target market. You may position your product/service for market success by concentrating on client demands, distinguishing your offering, and executing a well-planned launch strategy. To drive long-term development and profitability, continuously innovate and iterate depending on feedback and market insights.

Managing E-commerce and Fulfillment

Managing e-commerce and fulfillment is an essential part of establishing a profitable online business. It includes a variety of procedures and activities that assure effective order processing, inventory management, and timely product delivery to consumers. Businesses can create a flawless shopping experience, establish customer loyalty, and drive revenue growth by properly managing e-commerce and fulfillment processes.

Establishing a solid web platform is a critical component of managing e-commerce. This entails developing a user-friendly website or e-commerce store that displays products, gives thorough descriptions, and allows users to browse, choose, and purchase items with ease. To build trust and improve the customer's shopping experience, the website should be designed for mobile devices and offer safe payment methods.

Inventory management is critical in e-commerce businesses. It entails keeping track of stock levels, maintaining product availability, and reducing the possibility of overstocking or running out of popular products. Implementing inventory management systems or software may assist in automating and streamlining these procedures, allowing firms to maintain ideal stock levels and fulfill requests as quickly as possible.

Another important part of e-commerce administration is order processing. It entails receiving, verifying, and fulfilling consumer orders on time. By automating order routing, tracking, and customer contact, effective order management systems may assist speed this process. It is critical to develop trust and satisfaction by promptly recognizing orders, providing order progress updates, and delivering great customer service.

Efficient fulfillment is critical for correctly and on-time delivery of items to clients. This entails a number of procedures, including order selecting, packaging, and shipping. Investing in a well-organized fulfillment process, such as barcode or RFID technology for fast order picking, may help eliminate mistakes and increase fulfillment speed. Collaboration with dependable shipping carriers and improving shipment alternatives may help improve the customer experience while lowering shipping expenses.

Throughout the e-commerce and fulfillment processes, effective customer communication is critical. Clear and timely communication about order progress, shipment updates, and any delays assists in managing customer expectations and building confidence. Transparency and satisfaction may be improved by using automatic email alerts or a customer portal where consumers can follow their orders.

Returns and exchanges are an essential aspect of e-commerce operations. Having a clear and user-friendly return policy, simple return processes, and executing refunds or swaps quickly all contribute to customer satisfaction and loyalty. Returns handled efficiently assist to retain a favorable reputation and promote future purchases.

Monitoring and analyzing e-commerce and fulfillment indicators on a regular basis is critical for optimizing operations and identifying areas for development. Order processing speed, fulfillment accuracy, customer happiness ratings, and return rates are all key performance indicators (KPIs) that give significant insight into the success of e-commerce and fulfillment operations. Regularly evaluating these KPIs aids in the identification of bottlenecks, the streamlining of procedures, and the enhancement of the overall customer experience.

Finally, maintaining current on industry trends, developing technology, and customer preferences is critical to efficiently managing e-commerce and fulfillment. Adopting advances like automation, artificial intelligence, and data analytics may boost operational efficiency and consumer happiness.

Businesses may deliver a seamless shopping experience, establish customer loyalty, and drive growth in the competitive online marketplace by properly managing e-commerce and fulfillment processes. Prioritizing user-friendly platforms, rapid order processing, precise delivery, and good customer communication lays the groundwork for e-commerce success.

Chapter 10: Measuring Success and Analytics

Key Metrics and Performance Indicators

Key metrics and performance indicators are critical instruments for assessing a company's or project's success and effectiveness. These metrics give useful insights into numerous elements of operations, allowing for more informed decision-making and strategic planning. Businesses may discover areas of strength, find development possibilities, and measure progress toward their goals by monitoring and analyzing these indicators.

One of the most important measures to evaluate is revenue, which shows a company's financial performance. Revenue tracking aids in determining the organization's overall profitability and growth. Businesses can discover variables that contribute to swings in revenue by monitoring revenue patterns over time, such as seasonality or changes in consumer behavior.

Metrics for customer acquisition and retention are critical for determining the efficacy of marketing and customer interaction operations. Customer acquisition cost (CAC), customer lifetime value (CLV), and churn rate are metrics that offer information on the cost-effectiveness of obtaining new customers, their long-term worth, and the rate at which customers stop their relationship with the firm. These indicators assist firms in properly allocating resources and optimizing customer acquisition and retention tactics.

Conversion rates are critical measures of the success of marketing and sales activities. These metrics measure the proportion of website visitors or leads who complete the intended action, such as making a purchase, subscribing to a service, or filling out a form. Businesses may discover bottlenecks and modify their sales funnel to enhance conversion rates and drive revenue growth by tracking conversion rates at various phases of the customer experience.

Engagement indicators like website traffic, page views, and time spent on site give information on the amount of interest and involvement with a company's online presence. Analyzing these indicators allows organizations to assess how effective their content, user experience, and marketing initiatives are at attracting and engaging their target audience. Engagement indicators may help lead optimization efforts to improve website performance, user experience, and consumer engagement.

consumer satisfaction and feedback metrics assess consumer contentment and perceptions of a company's products or services. Net Promoter Score (NPS), customer satisfaction surveys, and online reviews give significant insights into consumer sentiment and assist in identifying areas for development. Businesses may improve their offers, solve consumer complaints, and develop closer relationships with their target audience by actively gathering and evaluating customer feedback.

Metrics of operational efficiency assess the efficacy and productivity of internal operations. These indicators might include order fulfillment time, customer service response time, or inventory turnover. Monitoring operational efficiency aids in the identification of bottlenecks, the streamlining of processes, the reduction of expenses, and the general improvement of corporate performance.

Financial measures such as gross profit margin, return on investment (ROI), and cash flow give information about a company's financial health and efficiency. These measures aid in the evaluation of profitability, liquidity, and the potential to create returns. Monitoring financial indicators assures the business's financial sustainability and aids in the direction of strategic financial choices.

It should be noted that the precise metrics and performance indicators recorded may differ based on the industry, corporate goals, and individual objectives. The main indicators chosen should be in line with the organization's strategic aims and give relevant insights into its performance and progress toward its objectives.

Businesses may make data-driven choices, discover areas for development, and measure progress toward their goals by constantly monitoring and evaluating important metrics and performance indicators. These indicators act as a compass, directing firms to success and offering a clear picture of their performance in a dynamic and competitive market.

Utilizing Analytics Tools and Platforms

Data-driven decision-making and company optimization need the use of analytics tools and platforms. Businesses may use these tools and platforms to gather, analyze, and interpret data to acquire useful insights into many parts of their operations. Businesses can make educated choices, uncover patterns and trends, and drive continuous improvement by leveraging the power of data.

Analytics tools and platforms enable organizations to collect and aggregate data from a variety of sources, including websites, social media platforms, customer databases, and sales systems. Customer behavior, website traffic, sales performance, marketing initiatives, and other information can all be included in this data. Businesses may gain a full perspective of their operations and make data-driven choices by centralizing data in one spot.

Once the data is acquired, analytics tools and platforms provide tremendous capabilities for data analysis and visualization. Businesses may employ statistical analysis, data mining, and machine learning algorithms to identify patterns, correlations, and insights that may not be obvious at first. Charts, graphs, and dashboards, for example, help stakeholders analyze complicated data and derive useful insights.

Businesses may acquire a comprehensive insight of client behavior and preferences by leveraging analytics tools and platforms. They can detect trends, client segmentation, and purchasing behaviors, enabling targeted marketing efforts and customised consumer experiences. Analyzing customer data also allows firms to better their client acquisition, retention, and loyalty tactics, resulting in increased income.

Additionally, analytics tools and platforms assist firms in optimizing their operational effectiveness. Businesses can discover bottlenecks, simplify operations, and save costs by examining data linked to inventory management, supply chain procedures, or manufacturing efficiency. These insights help firms to make data-driven decisions that improve resource allocation, productivity, and overall performance.

Analytics tools and platforms may dramatically boost marketing performance. Businesses can analyze the performance of various channels, messaging, or targeting methods by evaluating data connected to marketing initiatives. These analytics solutions provide insights that help firms optimize marketing expenditure, manage resources efficiently, and focus on the most successful techniques for reaching their target audience and driving conversions.

Analytics tools and platforms are also essential for tracking and assessing key performance indicators (KPIs). Businesses may analyze their performance, identify areas for development, and make data-driven modifications to their strategy by establishing appropriate metrics and tracking their progress over time. These solutions provide firms a real-time pulse on their performance, allowing them to remain nimble and adaptable in a volatile business climate.

Finally, good analytics tool and platform use enables firms to leverage the power of data for strategic decision-making, operational improvement, and business growth. Businesses may improve customer experiences, streamline processes, optimize marketing activities, and increase overall performance by utilizing data insights. Continuous use of analytics tools and platforms keeps firms nimble, competitive, and responsive to market developments and consumer requirements.

Adapting Strategies Based on Insights

The ability to adapt tactics based on insights is critical to corporate success and development. It entails making educated judgments and modifying current strategies to better match with changing conditions or accomplish targeted goals using data, feedback, and market intelligence. Businesses that are nimble and responsive may optimize their tactics, capitalize on opportunities, and effectively resolve obstacles.

Businesses must adopt a data-driven attitude in order to modify strategy based on findings. This entails gathering and evaluating pertinent data from a variety of sources, including customer feedback, market research, sales performance, and industry trends. Businesses may obtain significant insights into client preferences, market dynamics, and the efficiency of their present strategy by properly studying this data.

Businesses can discover areas where their plans may be falling short or where untapped possibilities exist by employing data and insights. Analyzing consumer feedback, for example, may indicate pain spots or unmet demands that may be addressed through product or service enhancements. Monitoring market trends and rival strategies, for example, might aid in identifying emerging opportunities or prospective dangers that require strategic revisions.

Businesses can establish action plans to change their strategy based on the insights gathered. Marketing campaigns may be refined, pricing methods adjusted, distribution networks optimized, or customer service offers enhanced. The purpose is to match plans with changing target audience demands and preferences, as well as market realities.

The process of adaptation necessitates a willingness to try and iterate. Businesses may receive real-time input and assess the impact of proposed changes by executing small-scale tests or pilots. This iterative technique enables for fast alterations and course corrections based on real-world implementation observations.

Continuous monitoring and measurement are required to assess the success of modified tactics. To analyze progress and success, businesses should define meaningful performance metrics and key performance indicators (KPIs). Regularly evaluating and analyzing these data offers useful input on the effectiveness of the modified techniques and aids in the identification of additional optimization possibilities.

When it comes to modifying tactics based on insights, flexibility and agility are essential. The business climate is fluid, and market circumstances may shift quickly. Being open to modifying and rewriting tactics based on new insights means that organizations may stay ahead of the competition.

During the adaptation phase, communication and collaboration within the company are critical. Sharing insights and analyses with key stakeholders such as marketing teams, sales teams, and executives develops a shared awareness of the need for strategy changes. Collaboration allows for a cohesive approach to change implementation, enabling consistent message and coordinated efforts across various areas.

It should be noted that insights can originate from a variety of sources, such as consumer feedback, market research, industry publications, and internal data. Businesses may acquire a full picture of the issues and opportunities they face by taking a holistic approach to acquiring insights. Combining qualitative and quantitative information offers a well-rounded picture of the issue and aids in making sound decisions.

Adapting strategies based on insights entails using data, feedback, and market intelligence to influence decision-making and adjust current tactics. Businesses may improve their plans, capture opportunities, and effectively handle problems by adopting a data-driven attitude, being nimble and responsive, and harnessing information from diverse sources. Continuous strategy adaption based on insights ensures that firms stay relevant, competitive, and capable of addressing changing consumer wants and market expectations.

Chapter 11: Staying Relevant and Evolving

Keeping Up with Social Media Trends

Keeping up with social media trends is critical for organizations and individuals alike to remain relevant and communicate with their target audience efficiently. Social media platforms are always changing, and new trends arise on a regular basis, altering how people consume and engage with material. Businesses can enhance their social media presence, generate engagement, and maintain a competitive advantage by remaining educated and modifying strategy to match with current trends.

To stay on top of social media trends, it's critical to continually watch and study the changing scene. Keep up with industry news, follow social media influencers, and participate in online forums where trends and best practices are discussed. By immersing yourself in these locations, you may learn about new features, algorithm modifications, popular content formats, and changing user habits.

Engaging with your target audience on social media platforms is a great method to learn about their preferences and remain up to date on their interests. Keep an eye on their remarks, engage in dialogues, and listen to their criticism. Listening to your audience will help you find patterns, preferences, and emerging subjects that will help define your content strategy and engagement strategies.

Explore and experiment with new features and formats introduced by social media sites. Live streaming, short-form films, tales, and augmented reality filters are all popular tools that may help businesses engage with their audiences in new and interesting ways. Maintain an open mind when it comes to experimenting with different forms and modifying your content strategy accordingly.

Collaborate with and learn from other social media providers and businesses in your field. Share views, ideas, and take part in cross-promotional events. Collaborations may help you reach new audiences, inspire you, and broaden your understanding of effective social media tactics. Engaging with other producers also contributes to the formation of a network that promotes mutual growth and keeps you in touch with the pulse of the social media community.

Understanding the success of your social media activities requires analyzing social media analytics and performance statistics. Review engagement rates, reach, follower growth, and other important data on a regular basis to uncover patterns and assess the effect of your content and tactics. This study might assist you in identifying patterns that are relevant to your audience and optimizing your content accordingly.

When it comes to keeping up with social media trends, being nimble and adaptable is essential. The social media world is always changing, and trends may shift swiftly. Maintain a flexible attitude, be open to experiment, and adapt your methods in response to new insights and feedback.

Continuous learning is essential for staying ahead of social media trends. Attend social media marketing seminars, workshops, or conferences to learn from industry leaders. Follow official blogs, documentation, or newsletters from social media platforms to stay up to speed on platform upgrades and algorithm adjustments. Seek out educational materials and remain up to date on developing trends and best practices.

Finally, assess and improve your social media strategy on a regular basis depending on your goals and the trends that correspond with your brand and target audience. Not every trend will be relevant to your company, so concentrate on those that connect with your brand values and consumer interests. A systematic strategy guarantees that you are efficiently harnessing social media trends to reach your unique goals.

Businesses may embrace opportunities, change their strategy, and interact with their audiences in meaningful ways by actively following social media trends. Maintaining a successful social media presence and generating engagement in an ever-changing digital world requires being educated, connecting with the target audience, experimenting with new features, and monitoring performance indicators.

Adapting to Algorithm Changes

Maintaining exposure and interaction on social media sites requires adapting to algorithm changes. Algorithms are continually changing, affecting how material is presented, ranked, and disseminated to people. Businesses may maximize their social media presence, reach their target audience, and successfully connect with their followers by understanding algorithm modifications and modifying strategy accordingly.

It's critical to remain up to speed on updates and changes from the social media sites themselves in order to respond to algorithm adjustments. Follow official blogs, sign up for newsletters, or join platform-specific groups to get information straight from the source. Platforms frequently give insights and advise on algorithm changes and how they may affect content exposure and engagement.

Regularly track stats and monitor the performance of your material. To discover trends and patterns, examine engagement rates, reach, impressions, and other relevant data. You may acquire insights into the particular adjustments that effect your content's exposure by examining how it performs before and after algorithm upgrades. This research may be used to lead changes in content generation and delivery methods.

Diversify your content formats and kinds to meet the needs of diverse users and platform features. Certain content forms or engagement patterns, such as video material or meaningful conversations, are frequently favored by algorithms. You may boost the likelihood of your content aligning with algorithmic preferences by adding a range of content forms into your plan. Experiment with various content kinds, including as videos, live streams, stories, or user-generated material, to see what connects most with your audience and is treated favorably by the algorithm.

Engage your audience in genuine conversation and develop meaningful engagement. Content that produces actual engagement and inspires dialogues is frequently prioritized by algorithms. Encourage your followers to leave comments, share your content, and tag others. Respond to comments and messages as soon as possible, and start dialogues to foster a feeling of community around your company. These interactions tell algorithms that your material is worthwhile and deserves to be seen more often.

Concentrate on offering your readers with high-quality and valuable material. Algorithms strive to produce material that consumers find interesting and relevant. Create material for your audience that informs, entertains, or inspires them. Avoid using clickbait or other low-quality strategies that may lead to poor user experiences. By publishing valuable information on a continuous basis, you enhance the probability of your content being favored by algorithms.

Create a consistent publishing schedule to maintain a continuous presence on social media channels. Accounts that are active and constant in their posting are frequently favored by algorithms. However, prioritize quality over quantity. Strive to strike a balance between offering useful material and sustaining constant audience engagement. Consistency aids believability by signaling to algorithms that your account is current and relevant.

Maintain agility and change your plans in response to real-time data and feedback. Monitor the performance of your material on a regular basis, study audience behavior, and be willing to make changes as needed. Be open to try new ideas, content formats, or distribution approaches in response to the most recent algorithm adjustments. Iterate and test to improve your strategy and align with changing algorithmic preferences.

It is vital to remember that algorithm modifications might differ between platforms and necessitate various adaption procedures. Each platform has its own set of algorithmic parameters that impact the visibility of information. Keep up to current on platform-specific updates and best practices to guarantee you can efficiently respond to changes on each platform.

Adapting to algorithm changes is a continuous process that demands alertness, adaptability, and a thorough knowledge of your target audience. Businesses may negotiate algorithm changes and retain exposure and engagement on social media platforms by remaining educated, evaluating performance indicators, diversifying content formats, cultivating participation, and continually offering high-quality material.

Expanding Your Influence Beyond Social Media

Extending your impact outside social media is a proactive strategy for broadening your reach, establishing your authority, and creating new chances outside of social media platforms. While social media is a tremendous platform for connection and engagement, broadening your influence allows you to reach out to new audiences and broaden your effect.

Content production outside of social media networks is one approach to broaden your reach. Consider launching a blog or website to publish long-form articles, in-depth insights, or lessons pertaining to your area of expertise. This allows you to demonstrate your expertise and position yourself as a thought leader in your sector. You can create a committed following and increase organic traffic to your website by continuously producing quality material on your own platform.

Another way to increase your impact is to take advantage of public speaking opportunities. Look for speaking opportunities, conferences, or industry events where you may share your knowledge with a live audience. Speaking engagements allow you to share your expertise, interact with like-minded people, and broaden your network. You may create trust and expand brand exposure outside social media channels by presenting powerful presentations.

Another effective strategy to increase your impact is to write a book or an e-book. Writing a book allows you to go deeper into your subject, give in-depth insights, and reach a larger audience. A published book boosts your reputation and establishes you as an expert in your subject. It expands your impact by opening doors to speaking engagements, media opportunities, and partnership requests.

Outside of social media, you may widen your impact by forming relationships and collaborations with other influencers, corporations, or organizations. Collaborations enable you to use one another's networks, cross-promote content, and reach new audiences. You may magnify your message and increase exposure outside social media platforms by collaborating with individuals or groups that have similar ideals or target audiences.

Using conventional media platforms, such as television, radio, or print magazines, can also help you increase your impact. Seek for chances for interviews, guest appearances, and expert commentary in the media. These channels offer more exposure and reach, allowing you to reach a larger audience and create reputation via reputable media outlets.

Another successful approach for expanding your reach outside social media is to create an email list or newsletter. Encourage your social media followers and website visitors to sign up for your newsletter, where you can send them special material, updates, and insights straight to their email. Creating a dedicated email list allows you to retain a direct connection with your audience and cultivate deeper relationships outside of social media.

Participating in offline community activities and events can also help you spread your influence. Attend industry conferences, local meetings, or seminars to network with others, offer your experience, and establish yourself as a useful resource. Offline engagements allow for face-to-face conversations, which aid in the development of trust and connection with your audience.

Remember to combine and cross-promote your social media presence with your other pursuits. Drive traffic to your blog, website, or speaking engagements using your other channels. Use your social media following to advertise your book or partnerships. You may increase your total reach and effect by generating synergy between your social media presence and your extended influence.

Extending your reach beyond social media necessitates a multifaceted approach that takes use of numerous channels, platforms, and chances. You can extend your influence, connect with new audiences, and create meaningful impact by diversifying your content creation, exploring speaking engagements, authoring books, establishing partnerships, leveraging traditional media, building an email list, engaging in offline activities, and integrating your social media presence.

Chapter 12: Building a Strong Personal Brand

Establishing Your Brand Identity

Building a great personal brand begins with establishing your brand identity. It entails identifying and articulating the core of who you are as a brand, what you stand for, and how you want your target audience to view you. Your brand identity establishes the tone for all interactions with your audience, molding their view and establishing a relationship with them.

Begin by outlining your brand values to develop your brand identity. These are the guiding concepts and ideals that serve as the foundation of your brand. Consider what you want to be recognized for, the guiding principles that guide your behavior, and the influence you want to have. You can guarantee that all parts of your brand match with these guiding principles by establishing your brand values.

Developing a distinctive brand identity entails creating a unified and recognized visual image. This includes creating a logo, picking a color palette, and selecting typefaces and visual components that reflect the personality of your business. Consistency in visual aspects makes it easier for your audience to recognize and remember your brand, enhancing brand recognition and recall.

Along with visual aspects, the tone and voice you employ in communication form your brand identity. Consider the language and writing style that best portrays the personality of your brand and resonates with your target audience. Your brand voice should be consistent across all platforms and touchpoints, whether it's welcoming, professional, authoritative, or conversational.

To properly develop your brand identity, you must constantly express your principles, aesthetic aspects, and brand voice. This consistency aids in the development of trust, promotes your brand's distinct character, and guarantees that your target audience identifies and remembers your brand.

Authenticity is critical in developing your brand identity. Stay loyal to who you are and what your brand represents. Communicate your principles and views openly, and allow your audience to see the true person behind the brand. Authenticity establishes a true relationship with your audience, generates trust, and distinguishes your business in a crowded social media field.

When developing your brand identity, keep your target audience in mind. Recognize their requirements, wants, and preferences, and link your brand identity with them. Customize your brand language and images to appeal to your target audience, ensuring that your brand identity speaks directly to their interests and goals.

Your brand's identity is not fixed. It may change as your brand expands and reacts to new market realities. Evaluate your brand identity on a regular basis to ensure it remains current and consistent with your goals and audience. Stay in sync with your audience's comments and be open to refining and improving your brand identity to better connect with them.

In conclusion, creating your brand identity is an important stage in developing a powerful personal brand. It entails identifying your brand values, designing a unified visual representation, and maintaining a consistent brand voice. The importance of authenticity and alignment with your target audience cannot be overstated. You can interact with your audience on a deeper level, generate trust, and differentiate yourself in the social media environment by developing a powerful and distinctive brand identity.

Developing Your Online Presence

Creating an online presence is an important part of building your brand and reaching your target audience in the digital age. It entails developing and improving numerous online platforms and channels in order to successfully promote your business, engage your audience, and make meaningful connections. Creating a great online presence necessitates a planned strategy and regular work to ensure that your brand is visible, accessible, and influential online.

Building a good website or blog is an important part of increasing your internet presence. Your website acts as a primary center for visitors to discover more about your company, explore its offers, and interact with its content. It should be aesthetically beautiful, user-friendly, and give relevant information that is consistent with your brand identity and the demands of your target audience. Search engine optimization improves your website's exposure and attracts organic visitors.

Social media networks are very important in growing your internet presence. Select the platforms that best represent your brand and target demographic, then maintain a constant presence on those channels. Create interesting profiles that mirror your brand's identity, and optimize them with important keywords and engaging descriptions. Publish high-quality material on a regular basis that connects with your audience and promotes conversation. You may establish a devoted community around your business by actively connecting with your audience through comments, messages, and debates.

Another important part of growing your internet presence is content development. Create relevant and entertaining content that showcases your knowledge, educates your readers, and solves their problems. Deliver consistent content that resonates with your brand values and meets the interests of your target audience, whether it's blog articles, videos, podcasts, or social media postings. Share your material on other platforms to broaden your reach and gain new fans.

Creating an online presence also entails building trust and authority in your business. Contribute to relevant online groups, forums, or industry-specific platforms where you may exchange knowledge, answer questions, and help others. Participating in debates and sharing your knowledge helps to establish trust and establishes you as an authority in your subject.

Creating a strong online presence necessitates consistent monitoring and analysis of your digital footprint. Keep track of brand-related web mentions, reviews, and comments. Respond quickly to both good and negative criticism to demonstrate your dedication to client satisfaction and boost your brand's reputation. Track the success of your online channels, monitor engagement, and obtain insights into audience behavior with analytics tools. This information assists you in refining your strategy, identifying areas for improvement, and making data-driven decisions.

When it comes to creating your internet presence, consistency is essential. Maintain a constant publishing schedule, reply quickly to messages and comments, and continuously produce excellent information. By being dependable, you build trust with your audience and improve your brand's existence.

Finally, cultivating ties with influencers, collaborators, and other companies can help to boost your online visibility. Participate in partnerships, collaborations, and cross-promotional projects that are consistent with your brand's values and target audience. Through affiliation with reputable partners, you may broaden your reach, reach new audiences, and develop credibility.

In short, improving your online presence entails constructing a professional website, maintaining a continuous presence on social media platforms, providing useful content, and communicating with your target audience. Building reputation, keeping an eye on your internet presence, and cultivating relationships with influencers and collaborators are all important. By deliberately creating your online presence, you may efficiently reach your target audience, generate a strong brand reputation, and engage with them in the digital world.

Engaging with Your Audience

Engaging your audience is a critical component of developing a strong online presence and maintaining genuine connections. It entails actively interacting, responding, and listening to your audience in order to foster a feeling of community, trust, and connections. Engaging your audience entails more than just conveying your message; it entails developing a discourse and a true relationship.

Responding to comments, mails, and enquiries as soon as possible is one strategy to engage your audience. Show gratitude for their remarks, respond to their queries, and resolve their problems as soon as possible. You indicate that you respect their feedback and are devoted to creating a meaningful connection with them by being responsive and attentive.

Initiating dialogues and promoting involvement is another excellent technique to engage your audience. Pose provocative questions, solicit feedback or experiences, and allow your audience to contribute their tales or ideas. You develop a feeling of community and make your audience feel valued and included by providing opportunities for debate.

Listening actively to your audience is an important part of engagement. Take note of their remarks, recommendations, and feedback. Take the time to learn about their wants, needs, and pain areas. You develop trust and deepen your relationship with them by proving that you actually care about their thoughts and viewpoints.

Personalization is essential for audience engagement. When possible, address your audience by name, customize your replies to their specific questions or remarks, and acknowledge their unique experiences. You make people feel seen and heard by demonstrating that you perceive and identify them as individuals, which strengthens their relationship to your brand.

Encourage the usage of user-generated content (UGC) as a form of interaction. Encourage your audience to contribute their brand-related experiences, stories, or inventions. Repost or share their UGC while crediting them and expressing gratitude for their work. You establish a feeling of ownership and pride in your community by including your audience in the development and marketing of content.

Being truthful and real while engaging with your audience is also required. Share behind-the-scenes footage, personal experiences, or difficulties you've experienced. By being transparent and vulnerable, you develop a stronger connection with your audience because they can relate to your experiences and perceive the genuineness of your brand.

Hosting live sessions, such as live Q&A sessions or webinars, is a good method to interact with your audience in real time. These interactive workshops provide direct connection as well as rapid response. Answer their questions, share your views, and create an engaging experience that enhances your relationship with your audience.

Social media platforms are not the only places where people may interact. Engage your audience through several methods, such as email newsletters, blog comments, or community forums. You may accommodate to varied tastes and guarantee that your audience can communicate with you in their chosen media by broadening your engagement efforts.

Finally, monitor and analyze engagement numbers on a regular basis to acquire insights into what connects with your audience. Keep track of likes, comments, shares, and other pertinent analytics to determine which material gets the most attention. Use this information to influence your content strategy, and concentrate on producing more of what your audience considers value.

To summarize, actively listening, reacting, and establishing meaningful connections with your audience is the essence of engaging them. You develop a true relationship with your audience by being responsive, personalizing your interactions, supporting user-generated content, and fostering transparency and authenticity. You may build a loyal and engaged audience that supports and contributes to the success of your business by cultivating a feeling of community, trust, and active debate.

Chapter 13: Expanding Your Reach through Influencer Marketing

Understanding Influencer Marketing

Understanding influencer marketing is critical for organizations and people trying to harness the power of social media and tap into the influence of well-known content providers. Collaboration with powerful individuals known as influencers who have developed reputation and a loyal following within a given niche or sector is what influencer marketing entails.

Influencer marketing, at its foundation, acknowledges the effect and reach that influencers have over their loyal audience. Influencers have earned the confidence and authority of their followers, who rely on their advice and knowledge. Businesses may get access to their engaged audience, improve brand recognition, and drive desired behaviors, such as product purchases or brand advocacy, by working with influencers.

It is critical to select the ideal influencers for your business while learning about influencer marketing. Begin by looking for influencers in your industry or niche who share your brand's values and target demographic. Look for influencers that have a genuine relationship with their following, good engagement rates, and a history of delivering high-quality content.

Collaborating with influencers entails forming mutually beneficial alliances. Define specific campaign goals and objectives that are consistent with your overall marketing strategy. Determine the form of partnership that best fits your aims and the influencer's abilities, such as sponsored content, product reviews, or brand ambassadorships. When addressing expectations, deliverables, and remuneration, effective communication and openness are critical.

Influencer marketing is about reaching the proper audience rather than a broad audience. Because followers of influencers trust their recommendations and opinions, their influence can lead to more focused and powerful engagements. When developing an influencer campaign, make sure the influencer's demographics, hobbies, and values match your target market.

This congruence contributes to your message's relevancy and effectiveness.

In influencer marketing, authenticity and openness are critical. To ensure openness and conform to regulatory rules, influencers should clearly declare their relationships and sponsored material. Authenticity is essential for maintaining trust between influencers and their followers. Encourage influencers to generate content that feels authentic and resonates with their audience while still communicating your brand's mission and values.

Influencer marketing is more than just one-time partnerships. Long-term connections with influencers may help you connect with their audience more deeply and achieve more consistent brand exposure. Consider cultivating relationships with influencers that sincerely believe in your company and its products/services, as these individuals may give continued support and advocacy.

Establish key performance indicators (KPIs) that are consistent with your campaign objectives to measure the effectiveness of influencer marketing. Reach, engagement rates, click-through rates, conversions, and brand perception are some examples. Analyze and evaluate campaign success on a regular basis to determine the return on investment (ROI) and make educated decisions about future influencer collaborations.

As the influencer marketing business grows, it is critical to keep current on industry trends, norms, and best practices. New laws or policies affecting influencer marketing are often introduced by social media networks and regulatory organizations. Stay educated, adjust your plans as needed, and follow ethical and compliance methods.

In summary, influencer marketing uses prominent content producers' influence and reach to promote products, services, or brand messaging. It entails discovering the proper influencers, forming genuine alliances, and tracking campaign performance. Understanding influencer marketing allows organizations to harness the power of trusted voices, broaden their reach, and connect with a specific and engaged audience.

Approaching Influencers

Approaching influencers is a critical step in carrying out effective influencer marketing campaigns and establishing meaningful collaborations. It's critical to contact influencers with a smart and planned approach that resonates with their interests, values, and audience. Here's a step-by-step guide to approaching influencers effectively.

To begin, undertake extensive research to find influencers relevant to your company and target demographic. Seek for influencers whose material is relevant to your business, specialty, or ideals. Consider the demographics of their followers, engagement rates, and the validity of their material. This research ensures that your approach is focused, increasing the likelihood of a good relationship.

Once you've discovered prospective influencers, take the time to learn about their job and develop a real connection with them. Learn about their material, follow them on social media, and interact with their updates. To show your interest and support, like, comment, and share their material. By really connecting with influencers, you create a connection and demonstrate your appreciation for their efforts.

Personalize your strategy when reaching out to influencers. Sending out generic, bulk communications should be avoided. Create unique remarks that highlight why you feel the partnership will be advantageous to both parties. Demonstrate that you have spent time learning about their brand and content. Mention particular publications or ads that piqued your interest, and explain how your business connects with their target demographic and values.

Explain your collaborative idea in a clear and comprehensive manner. Outline the campaign's goals, deliverables, and any expectations you may have. Give specifics about the pay or advantages you're providing, such as monetary remuneration, complimentary items, or exclusive access to events or activities. Your proposal's transparency and clarity assist influencers understand what they may anticipate from the relationship.

When connecting with influencers, underline the importance of their contribution to the collaboration. Showcase how their knowledge, honesty, and influence can help your brand. Demonstrate that you value their creative participation and are receptive to their suggestions. Influencers value collaborations that allow them to express their ideas while maintaining their own voice.

Throughout your correspondence, maintain a professional and courteous tone. Take into account the influencer's time and workload. Keep your messages brief and to the point, while yet expressing your excitement about the prospective partnership. Avoid being too forceful or demanding, since this can leave a bad impression and stymie the development of a strong working relationship.

If you do not receive an instant answer, follow up nicely. Influencers frequently receive several partnership requests, so it's conceivable that your original communication may be missed or overlooked. A pleasant follow-up communication demonstrates your sustained interest while also serving as a gently reminder.

Finally, after establishing a cooperation with an influencer, keep open and frequent communication channels open. Keep them informed of campaign developments, distribute important assets or information as soon as possible, and address any questions or issues they may have. Nurturing the relationship and providing a great experience for the influencer adds to a fruitful and long-term engagement.

In conclusion, addressing influencers involves extensive study, individualized communication, and genuine interest in their work. Be specific in your proposal, emphasize the value they offer to the cooperation, and keep a professional and courteous tone throughout. By engaging influencers deliberately and connecting with them on a personal level, you enhance the probability of successful partnerships that benefit both your business and the influencer.

Measuring Influencer Campaign Success

Measuring the performance of influencer initiatives is critical for assessing their impact, refining future plans, and demonstrating ROI to stakeholders. Measurement that is successful gives useful information into the performance of influencer partnerships and aids in determining the efficacy of your marketing initiatives. Here's a step-by-step guide to determining the effectiveness of an influencer campaign.

Defining clear and detailed marketing objectives is an important component of assessing influencer campaign performance. Establish quantifiable targets that match with your overall marketing objectives before commencing a campaign. These objectives might include raising brand exposure, increasing website traffic, increasing product sales, or enhancing engagement rates. Specific goals give a framework for assessing progress.

Track metrics like reach, impressions, and follower growth to determine the reach and exposure of your influencer marketing. These numbers represent the amount of distinct individuals who have been exposed to your brand's message via the influencer's content. Examine these figures to determine the overall reach of the campaign and if it met your goals.

Engagement metrics are critical in determining the efficiency of influencer collaborations. To gauge audience interaction with the material, track metrics such as likes, comments, shares, and video views. High levels of engagement show that the influencer's audience was responsive to the campaign and actively engaged with the material. To evaluate their success, compare these indicators to industry benchmarks or previous campaign results.

Tracking website traffic and conversions attributed to influencer marketing offers information about the campaign's impact on driving actions. To track traffic produced by influencer material, use techniques such as UTM parameters or affiliate tracking links. Analyze conversion rates, sales, or other targeted actions to measure the efficacy of the campaign in producing real outcomes for your company.

Another factor to consider when determining the effectiveness of an influencer campaign is brand sentiment. Monitor social media sentiment connected to the campaign to see how it changed your brand's impression. Tools like as social listening platforms or manual analysis of comments and mentions can assist in determining the overall attitude surrounding the campaign.

ROI is an important statistic for determining the financial effect of influencer initiatives. Calculate the ROI by comparing the campaign's expenditures, which include influencer remuneration, production expenses, and marketing costs, to the produced income or the projected worth of the campaign's effect. This offers a clear picture of the financial benefit of the influencer partnership.

In addition to quantitative measures, qualitative comments and insights from influencers themselves may provide significant views on campaign performance. Engage in open interactions with influencers to obtain feedback, learn about their audience's reaction, and receive insights into areas for future campaign enhancement. This qualitative input supplements quantitative indicators and aids in strategy refinement.

Continuous improvement requires regular reporting and analysis. Compile campaign data and insights into complete reports that give a thorough picture of campaign performance. Determine trends, patterns, and places where you may succeed or improve. Share these reports with stakeholders and use them to inform future influencer efforts.

To summarize, analyzing the performance of an influencer campaign entails establishing specific objectives, tracking reach, engagement, website traffic, conversions, brand sentiment, and ROI. Analyze quantitative and qualitative data to acquire a complete picture of the campaign's impact. Regular reporting and analysis give insights for optimizing future influencer engagements and showing to stakeholders the effectiveness of influencer marketing.

Chapter 14: Harnessing the Power of Video Content

The Rise of Video Content

The emergence of video content has transformed the way people consume and exchange information online. Video has developed as a potent medium for capturing audiences, emotionally engaging them, and delivering messages in a more dynamic and immersive manner. Its popularity has skyrocketed, altering social networking platforms, marketing methods, and the digital world as a whole.

The potential of video content to transmit messages more effectively than other kinds of media is one of the primary elements driving its development. Videos mix visual and audio aspects to provide viewers with a rich and engaging experience. This multi-sensory technique makes it simpler to grab people's attention, elicit emotions, and present information in a memorable way.

Video content also aids storytelling, allowing companies and producers to express storylines and engage with people on a more personal way. Videos may elicit emotions, ignite conversations, and develop a strong brand identity via the use of graphics, sound, and narrative structure. Brands can use the power of narrative in video content to express their values, engage their audience, and establish a devoted following.

The widespread availability of high-quality recording equipment, editing software, and user-friendly video sharing sites has aided the proliferation of video content. Anyone with a smartphone or camera may make and share movies, democratizing content creation and delivery. This ease of access has enabled individuals and businesses to use video to express themselves, exchange knowledge, and reach a worldwide audience.

By adding video capabilities and emphasizing video content in users' feeds, social media companies have embraced the video revolution. Platforms such as YouTube, TikTok, Instagram, and Facebook have evolved into video consumption and discovery hotspots. These platforms provide a variety of video formats, such as short-form videos, live streaming, narrative, and long-form material, to accommodate a wide range of audience tastes.

The popularity of video content has also had an impact on marketing methods. Brands have understood the power of video in captivating attention, communicating messages, and driving conversions. Brand promotion, product debuts, and narrative projects have all benefited from video marketing campaigns. Marketers use video to engage consumers, raise brand recognition, and create leads.

In addition, the emergence of video material has altered how instructional content is consumed and provided. Online courses, tutorials, and instructional films have all grown in popularity as ways to share information and skills. Video helps instructors to visually show procedures, engage students with interactive aspects, and deliver an immersive learning experience.

Live video streaming has become an important part of the video content ecosystem. Individuals and companies may engage with their audiences in real time through live streaming, allowing for quick contact, feedback, and community development. Live video provides an honest and unedited experience that fosters openness and trust.

The proliferation of video content has had a significant influence on user behavior and internet consumption patterns. Because videos are more entertaining, time-efficient, and easily shareable, audiences are increasingly preferring video content over text-based alternatives. The proliferation of mobile devices and enhanced internet access has increased demand for on-the-go video entertainment.

Finally, the emergence of video content has altered the digital world, transforming how information is received, shared, and promoted. Video has become a dominant force in social media, marketing, education, and entertainment due to its capacity to fascinate, engage, and communicate messages. As video evolves and expands in significance, its role in molding online communication and narrative will only rise.

Creating Engaging Video Content

In the digital era, creating captivating video content has become increasingly valuable. Engaging films captivate viewers' attention, elicit emotions, and leave a lasting impression. Creating great video content is vital for connecting with your audience and accomplishing your goals, whether you're a company, content publisher, or individual.

It is critical to begin with a clear aim when creating entertaining video content. Determine whether your video's goal is to educate, entertain, inspire, or advertise a product or service.

Understanding your goal allows you to tailor the content and structure of your video accordingly.

The essence of entertaining video content is storytelling. Create a story that connects with your audience, elicits emotions, and keeps them engaged from beginning to end. Create an engaging tale, intriguing people or components, and tension, surprise, or an emotional connection. A well-written narrative will capture your audience and leave an indelible impact.

Visual appeal is important in creating interesting video material. Take note of your video's aesthetics, such as its composition, lighting, colors, and overall visual style. Create aesthetically attractive moments that enrich the tale and draw the spectator in. Use pictures artistically to communicate information, set the tone, or generate suspense.

Use sound and music to increase the emotional impact of your video. Select background music that suits your video's tone and narrative. Strategically use sound effects to provide depth and engage viewers in the experience. Audio components that are well-chosen and well-placed may dramatically improve the engagement and overall quality of your movie.

Take into account the length and timing of your video. In today's fast-paced digital world, shorter films tend to perform better in capturing and retaining viewers' attention. Maintain a consistent tempo throughout the film, with a balance of dynamic and calmer periods to keep viewers engaged. Edit your video with care to remove any extraneous stuff while maintaining a compact and effective narrative.

Incorporate interactive components into your video material to engage your visitors. Include call-to-actions, interactive polls, or suggestions for comments and sharing to encourage visitors to participate. This motivates viewers to participate and take action, increasing engagement and establishing a feeling of community around your content.

Creating interesting video content requires authenticity. Be honest, relatable, and loyal to the principles and characteristics of your brand. Audiences value authenticity and are more inclined to engage with information that appears genuine and genuine. Showing the human aspect of your company or sharing personal tales might help you connect with your audience on a deeper level.

To keep your material fresh and interesting, experiment with multiple video formats and styles. To increase visual appeal, try using animations, motion graphics, or special effects. To appeal to varied audience interests and keep their attention, vary the sorts of films you generate, such as instructional, behind-the-scenes footage, interviews, or narrative videos.

Finally, keep an eye on the metrics and feedback on your video material. To evaluate how your films are performing, examine indicators such as view counts, watch time, engagement rates, and audience retention. Utilize this information to iterate and improve your future content. Listen to your viewers' opinions, comments, and ideas as well to better grasp their preferences and expectations.

In summary, developing engaging video content entails establishing your goal, constructing a captivating plot, paying attention to visual appeal and sound, keeping an appropriate duration and pace, including interactive aspects, being authentic, and experimenting with various forms. Analyze data on a regular basis and listen to audience input to modify and improve your material. You can connect with your audience, create a lasting impression, and achieve your goals by making entertaining films.

Leveraging Live Video and Streaming

Using live video and streaming to engage people in real-time and create meaningful connections has become a strong tool. Live video allows you to communicate directly with viewers, share your experiences, and develop a feeling of community. Live video may be a significant complement to your content strategy when utilized carefully, allowing you to reach and engage your audience in a more immediate and immersive manner.

One of the most significant advantages of live video is its capacity to instill a feeling of urgency and exclusivity. Live broadcasts take place in real time, giving viewers a sense of immediacy that motivates them to tune in and interact. You may increase attendance and develop interest by advertising and publicizing forthcoming live sessions in advance.

Live video provides for quick audience connection and participation. Viewers may remark, ask questions, and offer comments in real time, making the experience lively and participatory. This two-way communication allows you to interact with your audience more deeply and answer to their questions or comments in real time. It's a chance to have important dialogues, resolve problems, and make viewers feel heard and respected.

Live video is a great way to provide behind-the-scenes information, exclusive access, or live events. It allows visitors to witness the true and unedited parts of your content development process, events, or daily operations by providing a window into your world or business. Transparency may help you connect with your audience and develop trust.

It is critical to plan and prepare when using live video to create a seamless and interesting experience. Outline the main subjects or ideas you want to address, and prepare a broad script or talking points to lead your live session. Be adaptable and receptive to unexpected moments and exchanges with your audience. Authenticity is essential, so don't be scared to express yourself and allow your true self come through.

To optimize exposure and engagement, promote your live sessions via your social media platforms and other communication channels. Tell your viewers when and where the live video will take place, as well as why they should watch. Schedule your live sessions around times when your audience is most engaged and likely to be accessible to watch.

A good live video experience requires engaging images and excellent audio. Ascertain that you have a reliable internet connection, enough lighting, and decent audio quality. Pay attention to your surrounds and build a visually appealing arrangement that represents the style and message of your company. To ensure a professional and comfortable watching experience, make sure your voice is clear and any background noise is eliminated.

After your live video concludes, make the recording available to anyone who were unable to see it live. Upload the video to your social media channels, website, or other platforms to repurpose it. This allows a larger audience to interact with the information and guarantees that the value of the live session goes beyond the live broadcast.

Finally, examine the results and feedback from your live videos. Take note of indicators such as viewership, engagement rates, comments, and shares. Examine what went well and what may be improved for future live sessions. Listen to your audience's comments and adopt them to improve the overall experience and adapt to their preferences.

In conclusion, utilizing live video and streaming provides a one-of-a-kind opportunity to engage and connect with your audience in real-time. It stimulates engagement and gives a genuine view into your life by creating a sense of immediacy. Plan and prepare for live sessions, market them ahead of time, and provide interesting images and clear audio. Analyze performance and feedback to develop and optimize your live video approach over time. You can create unique experiences, strengthen connections, and improve your entire content strategy by using the power of live video.

Conclusion

As we near the end of our transforming voyage through the realm of social media influence, we ponder the information learned, the friendships made, and the limitless possibilities that await us. We've dived into the complexities of social media, developing personal brands, connecting with audiences, and growing our reach through influencer marketing throughout this book.

The effect of social media has altered our digital world, providing individuals and companies with a never-before-seen platform to connect, inspire, and make a difference. We investigated the emergence of social media influencers, learning how to define niches, create interesting content, and establish engaged groups.

Choosing the correct platforms and using their distinct capabilities has resulted in limitless possibilities. We assessed several social media networks, focused on major platforms, and investigated supplemental channels that magnify our messaging. We have created fascinating online personalities that appeal with viewers by mastering the art of storytelling, using images, and embracing the authenticity of our voices.

Our path has brought us through the complexities of partnerships and collaborations, where we contacted companies carefully, negotiated contracts, and kept our brand connections real. As we increase our reach and effect, we have utilized the power of affiliate marketing and sponsorships, always keeping disclosure and ethical issues in mind.

As we found lucrative concepts, built solutions, and negotiated the world of e-commerce and delivery, we were able to make an indelible impression by creating our own products and services. We monitored our success, altered tactics based on insights, and remained adaptable in a changing digital world by using essential metrics and analytics.

With our gaze fixed on the horizon, we recognize the significance of being relevant and developing. We've investigated the ever-changing social media trends, responded to algorithm adjustments, and broadened our reach outside the confines of social media platforms.

As we formed our brand identities, grew our online presence, and connected genuinely with our audiences, developing a strong personal brand has been a cornerstone of our journey. We've harnessed the power of live video and streaming, taking advantage of the immersive experience it provides to engage with our viewers in real time.

As we come to the end of this transforming journey, we are reminded that social media influence is more than simply numbers, likes, or followers—it is about leaving a lasting impression, building meaningful relationships, and inspiring good change. In a digital age that desires true human connection, it is the essence of our creativity, sincerity, and enthusiasm.

It is now time to go on your own unique path, armed with information, motivation, and a road map to success. Accept the power of social media influence, let your imagination run wild, and write your own chapter in the ever-changing saga of digital influence.

Keep in mind that the trip does not finish here. The world of social media influence is dynamic, ever-changing, and full of almost infinite opportunities. Accept your lessons, adjust to new trends, and allow your voice to resound with authenticity and impact.

Thank you for joining us on this incredible journey. May your path be enlightened, your impact be significant, and your narrative continue to inspire others in the extraordinary world of social media influence.